Studies of Research on Social Work Practice:
A Bibliography

Harriett M. Bartlett Practice Effectiveness Project
Lynn Videka-Sherman, Project Director

National Association of Social Workers, Inc.
Silver Spring, Maryland

Copyright © 1986, National Association of Social Workers, Inc.

All rights reserved. No part of this book may be reproduced or transmitted in any form or by any means, electronic or mechanical, including photocopying, recording, or by any information storage and retrieval system, without permission in writing from the publisher.

Library of Congress Cataloging-in-Publication Data

Studies of research on social work practice.
   At head of title: Harriett M. Bartlett Practice Effectiveness Project.
   I. Social service—Bibliography. 2. Social service—Research—Bibliography. I. Videka-Sherman, Lynn, 1951–   . II. National Association of Social Workers. III. Harriett M. Bartlett Practice Effectiveness Project.
Z7164.C4S78 1986 [HV40]   016.361′0072   86-20806
ISBN 0-87101-146-8

Printed in the U.S.A.

Contents

Foreword	iv
Introduction	1
Bibliography	
Child Welfare	5
Children's Behavioral/Emotional Problems	8
Community Intervention	19
Corrections	19
Developmental Disabilities	20
Family Treatment	23
Gerontology	26
Health	31
Mental Health	34
Organizational Effectiveness	45
Public Social Services	47
Substance Abuse	50
Unemployment	55
Appendix	57

Foreword

THE HARRIETT M. BARTLETT Practice Effectiveness Project was born out of a great tradition in social work—the delineation and clarification of social work practice. It was conceived as an opportunity for the social work profession to continue its consolidation of theory and practice, to determine the state of professional knowledge and methods, and to project areas that require clarification. Many earlier and ongoing efforts within NASW—from workshops and publications on the development of conceptual frameworks for the profession, to the definition of clinical social work and specialization, to the identification of research needs, and to the establishment of an online abstracts database—contributed to the shape and substance of the project as well as to the advancement of social work practice.

The major functions of the Bartlett project were designed as follows:

1. To pave the way for the establishment of a national clearinghouse on social work practice research, which would include data files on all completed studies, research in progress, investigations and organizations, and bibliographies.

2. To analyze practice studies for their practice-effectiveness elements, with the objective of compiling all valid information for use by practitioners.

3. To evaluate and clarify data on practice effectiveness through the interaction of small peer groups, with the objective of consolidating the definitions pertinent to social work knowledge and practice.

4. To project significant areas of needed and potentially productive research.

Inevitably, as the project became a reality, some changes took place in its functions, management, and operations. Now, the results of the project have been made available, first through a detailed report presented at a meeting during the 1985 NASW Professional Symposium and then in this publication of the bibliography of studies and research on social work practice used in the project analysis.

Many next steps still remain to be taken to engage an even-broader group of professionals in the task of obtaining information about outcomes of practice. NASW would be pleased to receive information and suggestions from researchers and practitioners about their work in this area, as well as suggestions for continuing the clarification and development of the social work knowledge base.

CHAUNCEY A. ALEXANDER
Huntington Beach, California

August 1986

Introduction

THE CONTEXT IN WHICH this bibliography was developed and produced was described at the 1985 NASW Professional Symposium in Chicago in a detailed report by the project director and committee representatives of the Harriett M. Bartlett Practice Effectiveness Project. The rationale for the project was rooted in the efforts of the National Association of Social Workers and its predecessor organizations to come to grips with the problems of developing a unified profession of social work and its corollary, that is, identifying and clarifying what social workers do—questions that have been addressed ever since Abraham Flexner threw down the gauntlet at the National Conference of Charities and Correction in 1915 by declaring that social work was not a profession. For those who continue to find these questions worth pursuing, as well as to set the work of the Bartlett project in its proper context, it may be useful to review some of the history of the study of social work practice and its effectiveness.

The first landmark effort was the 1929 report of the Milford Conference, which developed a description of the content of "generic" social casework and identified the differences and similarities among the various specialties recognized in the profession at that time. In 1950, the National Council on Social Work Education (forerunner of the Council on Social Work Education) commissioned Ernest V. Hollis and Alice Taylor Davis to help decide "what social work is and what it is not." Hollis and Taylor came up with a statement that described social work as a *helping* activity, a *social* activity, and a *liaison* activity; presented a statement of social work objectives; and framed seven questions by which to evaluate social work and social work education.[1]

In 1958 and subsequently, NASW, through the efforts of its Commission on Practice (chaired by Harriett M. Bartlett), developed a statement called "The Working Definition of Social Work Practice." The commission intended it to be revised, reworked, and redefined as times—and the profession—changed. In 1959, CSWE issued an extensive 12-volume study of social work education in the United States, which dealt with the goals, functions, and definition of social work and its specializations and proposed a theoretical framework.[2]

Although interest in the subject of defining and clarifying social work practice has ebbed and flowed over time, a number of events took place and a body of literature began to accumulate whose direction pointed more and more to the concept of social functioning and the interaction

---

[1] E. V. Hollis and A. T. Davis, *Social Work Education in the United States* (New York: Columbia University Press, 1951).

[2] W. W. Boehm, *Social Work Curriculum Study* (New York: Council on Social Work Education, 1959).

between the client and the environment as key to these questions. A summary of crucial dates and publications showing this direction may be found in the Appendix.

Following the publication of Bartlett's *The Common Base of Social Work Practice* in 1970, the NASW Publications Committee continued to probe the problems and needs of the profession as one focus of NASW's publishing program. With Harriett Bartlett's assistance—both intellectual and financial—the committee undertook discussions, meetings, and publications on the purpose, mission, and activities of social work—what they are and what they should be. This work ultimately led to the publication of two issues of *Social Work* on conceptual frameworks and contributed to the establishment of specialty journals within the publications program, as well as to the development of an online database as part of *Social Work Research and Abstracts.*

During this period, NASW and CSWE began to collaborate on the thorny problem of social work specialization. In addition, with the help of the National Institute of Mental Health, NASW called together, in a conference on The Future of Social Work Research, the leading social work researchers in the country to try to stimulate a plan for developing the knowledge necessary to improve the delivery of social work services. Their recommendation, among others, was that NASW should establish a clearinghouse for social work research.

All these activities gave birth to the notion that a system was needed to collect information about *effective* social work practice and that some way should be found to feed it back to practitioners. Harriett Bartlett agreed to provide a modest grant to get such a system started. The first step was to identify and assemble studies that had been done on social work practice. This collection of studies could then form the base for the future establishment of a clearinghouse that could monitor and stimulate research and, ultimately, build a capacity in a national organization—NASW—for filling the gaps.

In the early 1980s, an NASW committee (Chauncey Alexander, chair; Edith Freeman; Bernice Harper; Beatrice Saunders; and Eugene Shinn) was appointed to carry responsibility for initiating the Practice Effectiveness Project and for setting its goals and direction. Lynn Videka-Sherman, the project director, was responsible for its execution and outcome. The full scope of the project, of which this bibliography is one piece, is presented in the final report.[3] During the course of the project, 745 citations were identified as reporting systematic research on social work practice, and these were included in the bibliography. As stated in the final report:

---

[3] "Report to the NASW Board of Directors by the Harriett M. Bartlett Practice Effectiveness Project," Lynn Videka-Sherman, project director. Unpublished manuscript, National Association of Social Workers, Silver Spring, Maryland, July 10, 1985.

Studies were included in the bibliography providing that
  1. They reported results of systematic, qualitative, or quantitative research on social work practice;
  2. The practitioners were social workers (BSW, MSW, doctorate) or an interdisciplinary team that included social workers;
  3. The service was delivered under the auspices of a social service agency (e.g., public welfare agency or family service agency) even when the practitioners were not trained social worker. (e.g., peer counselors).[4]

Out of this larger group of studies, those in mental health (pp. 00-00 of this bibliography) were subjected to specific data analysis as part of one of the project's goals to identify factors associated with effective social work practice. The project's staff utilized a research approach called meta-analysis—an approach not used before in the field of social work research—in carrying out the analysis.[5] The final number of studies fully analyzed was 142 of which 94 (those with comparison groups) "were used for analysis of correlates of effective practice."[6]

The bibliography is organized by major areas of practice (such as health, mental health, and public welfare). This schema is not intended to define fields of practice for the profession; rather, it is used simply as an organizing mechanism for this project. The Harriett M. Bartlett Project Advisory Committee hopes that this bibliography will prove useful to the profession and provide one more step on the road to the development of a comprehensive resource in the area of practice research.

BEATRICE N. SAUNDERS
New York, New York

August 1986

---

[4] Ibid., pp. 8-9.
[5] Ibid., p. 12.
[6] Ibid., p. 37.

BIBLIOGRAPHY

Child Welfare

Aldridge, M. J., and Cautley, P. W. "The Importance of Worker Availability in the Functioning of New Foster Homes." *Child Welfare,* 54 (June 1975), pp. 444–453.

Allerhand, M. E.; Weber, R. E.; and Haug, M. *Adaptation and Adaptability: The Beliefane Follow-Up Study.* New York: Child Welfare League of America, 1966.

Amiung, S. *An Ounce of Prevention: A Survey of Preventive Service Programs Contracted by New York City Special Services for Children.* New York: Clark (Robert Sterling) Foundation, May 1981.

Barth, R. P., et al. "Self-Control Training with Maltreating Parents." *Child Welfare,* 62 (April 1983), pp. 313–323.

Boyd, L. H., and Remy, L. L. "Is Foster-Parent Training Worthwhile?" *Social Service Review,* 52 (June 1978), pp. 275–296.

———. "Foster Parents Who Stay Licensed and the Role of Training." *Journal of Social Service Research,* 2 (Winter 1979), pp. 373–387.

Burch, G., and Mohr, V. "Evaluating a Child Abuse Intervention Program." *Social Casework: The Journal of Contemporary Social Work,* 61 (February 1980), pp. 90–99.

Bush, M. "Institutions for Dependent and Neglected Children: Therapeutic Option of Choice or Last Resort?" *American Journal of Orthopsychiatry,* 50 (April 1980), pp. 239–255.

Campbell, S. B., et al. "Successful Foster Homes Need Parent-Child Match." *Journal of Social Welfare,* 6 (Winter 1979–80), pp. 49–60.

Claburn, W. E., and Magura, S. "Administrative Case Review for Foster Children." *Social Work Research and Abstracts,* 14 (Spring 1978), pp. 34–40.

Cohn, A. H. "Effective Treatment of Child Abuse and Neglect." *Social Work,* 24 (September 1979), pp. 513–519.

Cohn, A. H., and DeGraaf, B. "Assessing Case Management in the Child Abuse Field." *Journal of Social Service Research,* 5, No. 1/2 (1982), pp. 29–43.

Community Research Applications. *Child Abuse and Neglect Programs: Practice and Theory.* Washington, D.C.: U.S. Department of Health, Education & Welfare, 1977.

Conte, J. R.; Berliner, L.; and Nolan, D. "Police and Social Worker

Cooperation: A Key in Child Sexual Assault Cases." *FBI Law Enforcement Bulletin,* 49, No. 3 (1980), pp. 7–10.

Costanzo, W. "Improving Knowledge and Attitudes About Child Abuse: A Comparison of Two Parenting-Training Treatments of Adolescents." *International Child Welfare Review,* 41 (June 1979), pp. 35–41.

Elmer, E. "Abused Children and Community Resources." *International Journal of Offender Therapy,* 1 (April 1967), pp. 16–23.

Euster, S., and Noble, L. S. "A Unique Approach to Foster Training: Preparing Caseworkers as Instructors." *Journal of Continuing Social Work Education,* 1, No. 2 (1981), pp. 7–10, 32, and 34.

Fanshel, D. "Parental Visiting of Children in Foster Care: Key to Discharge." *Social Service Review,* 49 (December 1975), pp. 493–514.

Franklin, D. S., and Massarik, F. "The Adoption of Children with Medical Conditions: Part I—Process and Outcome." *Child Welfare,* 48 (October 1969), pp. 459–467.

————. "The Adoption of Children with Medical Conditions: Part II—The Families Today." *Child Welfare,* 48 (November 1969), pp. 533–539.

Freund, V. W. "Evaluation of a Self-Approval Method for Inducting Foster Parents." *Smith College Studies in Social Work,* 46 (March 1976), pp. 115–126.

Johnston, B. J. *A Team Approach to Child Abuse Intervention: Some Preliminary Findings.* Minneapolis, Minn.: Midwest Sociological Society, 1979.

Jones, M. A. "Reducing Foster Care Through Services to Families." *Children Today,* 5 (November–December 1976), pp. 6–10.

Jones, M. A.; Newman, R.; and Shyne, A. W. *A Second Chance For Families: Evaluation of a Program to Reduce Foster Care.* New York: Child Welfare League of America, 1976.

Kirst, M., et al. *State Services for Children: An Exploration of Who Benefits, Who Governs.* New York: Bank Street College of Education, 1979.

Lahti, J. "A Follow-Up Study of Foster Children in Permanent Placements." *Social Service Review,* 56 (December 1982), pp. 556–571.

Lewis, H.; Jahn, J.; and Bishop, J. A. *Designing More Effective Protective Services: Intervening in the Recurrence Cycle of Neglect and Abuse of Children. Phase I: Report on the Philadelphia Child Welfare Project, 1965–67.* Philadelphia: University of Pennsylvania School of Social Work Research Center, 1967.

Magura, S. "Clients View Outcomes of Child Protective Services." *Social Casework: The Journal of Contemporary Social Work,* 63 (November 1982), pp. 522-531.

———. "Trend Analysis in Foster Care." *Social Work Research and Abstracts,* 15 (Winter 1979), pp. 29-36.

McCabe, A. *The Pursuit of Promise.* New York: Community Service Society, 1967.

Mech, E. V. "Child Welfare Research: A Review and Critique." *The Annals,* 355, No. 5 (1964), pp. 20-30.

Oppenheimer, A. "Triumph over Trauma in the Treatment of Child Abuse." *Social Casework,* 59 (June 1978), pp. 352-358.

Pecora, P. J., and Gingerich, W. J. "Worker Tasks and Knowledge Utilization in Group Child Care: First Findings." *Child Welfare,* 60 (April 1981), pp. 221-231.

Pratt, C. "Foster Parents as Agency Employees." *Children,* 13 (January–February 1966), pp. 14-15.

Rapp, C. A. "Effect of the Availability of Family Support Services on Decisions About Child Placement." *Social Work Research and Abstracts,* 18 (Spring 1982), pp. 21-27.

Rosen, H. "How Workers Use Cues to Determine Child Abuse." *Social Work Research and Abstracts,* 17 (Winter 1981), pp. 27-33.

Rubenstein, H. "After Care, Who Cares?" *Child Welfare,* 46 (April 1967), pp. 195-202.

Shapiro, D. *Parents and Protectors: A Study in Child Abuse and Neglect.* New York: Child Welfare League of America, 1979.

Sherman, E. A., et al. *Service to Children in Their Own Homes: Its Nature and Outcome.* New York: Child Welfare League of America, 1973.

Simon, R. D., and Simon, D. K. "The Effect of Foster Parent Selection and Training on Service Delivery." *Child Welfare,* 61 (September–October 1982), pp. 515-524.

Smith, A. N., and Spence, C. M. "National Day Care Study: Optimizing the Day Care Environment." *American Journal of Orthopsychiatry,* 50 (October 1980), pp. 718-721.

Stein, T. J. "Early Intervention in Foster Care." *Public Welfare,* 34 (Spring 1976), pp. 38-44.

Stein, T. J.; Gambrill, E. D.; and Wiltse, K. T. *Children in Foster Homes.* New York: Praeger Publishers, 1978.

8 / Bibliography

———. "Dividing Case Management in Foster Family Cases." *Child Welfare*, 56 (May 1977), pp. 321–331.

Sundel, M., et al. "The Self-Assessment Manual: A Strategy to Improve Local Child Welfare Services." *Child Welfare*, 59 (December 1980), pp. 625–636.

Wolfe, D. A.; Sandler, J.; and Kaufman, K. A. "Competency-Based Parent Training Program for Child Abusers." *Journal of Counseling and Clinical Psychology*, 49 (October 1981), pp. 633–640.

Wolock, I. "Community Characteristics and Staff Judgments in Child Abuse and Neglect Cases." *Social Work Research and Abstracts*, 18 (Summer 1982), pp. 9–15.

Young, L. R. "An Interim Report on an Experimental Program of Protective Service." *Child Welfare*, 45 (July–August 1966), pp. 373–381 and 387.

Children's Behavioral/Emotional Problems

Baggish, R. C., et al. "Quality Assurance in a Children's Psychiatric Hospital." *Administration in Mental Health*, 8 (Spring 1981), pp. 194–201.

Banchy, N., and Canter, A. "A Home-Based Parent Education Program." *Social Work in Education*, 1 (Winter 1979), pp. 36–46.

Barcai, A., et al. "A Comparison of Three Group Approaches to Under-Achieving Children." *American Journal of Orthopsychiatry*, 43 (January 1973), pp. 133–141.

Bardill, D. R. "Group Therapy Techniques with Pre-adolescent Boys in a Residential Training Center." *Child Welfare*, 52 (September–October 1973), pp. 533–541.

Beckham, C. O.; Johnston, L.; and Beckham, E. "Sex Education for Children in a Residential Center." *Child Welfare*, 58 (June 1979), pp. 393–402.

Bell, C. A.; Casto, G.; and Daniels, D. S. "Ameliorating the Impact of Teen-age Pregnancy on Parent and Child." *Child Welfare*, 62 (February 1983), pp. 167–173.

Berleman, W. C.; Seaberg, J. R.; and Steinburn, T. W. "The Delinquency Prevention Experiment of the Seattle Atlantic Street Center: A Final Evaluation." *Social Service Review*, 46 (September 1972), pp. 323–346.

Berleman, W. C., and Steinburn, T. W. "The Execution and Evaluation of a Delinquency Prevention Program." *Social Problems*, 14 (Spring 1967), pp. 413–423.

Blizinsky, M. J., and Reid, W. J. "Problem Focus and Change in a Brief-Treatment Model." *Social Work,* 25 (March 1980), pp. 89-93.

Block, J. "Effects of a Rational-Emotive Mental Health Program on Poorly Achieving, Disruptive High School Students." *Journal of Counseling Psychology,* 25 (January 1978), pp. 61-65.

Bohnstedt, M. "Answers to Three Questions About Juvenile Diversion." *Journal of Research in Crime Delinquency,* 15 (February 1978), pp. 109-123.

Browning, R. M. "Behavior Therapy for Stuttering in a Schizophrenic Child." *Behaviour Research and Therapy,* 5, No. 1 (1967), pp. 27-35.

Broxmeyer, N. "Practitioner-Research in Treating a Borderline Child." *Social Work Research and Abstracts,* 14 (Winter 1978), pp. 5-10.

Bruck, M. "An Evaluation of the Use of Group Treatment for 'Hard-to-Reach' Latency-Age Children in a Community Guidance Clinic." *Child Welfare,* 45 (July-August 1966), pp. 395-403.

Calhoun, N. "Social Awareness Group for Girls with Poor Self-Concept." *School Social Work Journal,* 3 (Spring 1979), pp. 110-115.

Cantoni, L. *Eighteen Family Life Education Groups Conducted for Parents by Family Service of Metropolitan Detroit.* Detroit: Family Service of Metropolitan Detroit, 1970.

Caplan, N. "Treatment Intervention and Reciprocal Interaction Effects." *Journal of Social Issues,* 24 (March 1968), pp. 63-88.

Cimler, E. R. *1976 Evaluation Report.* St. Paul: Child Development Centers of Minnesota, 1976.

Cline, D. W. "Video Tape Documentation of Behavioral Change in Children." *American Journal of Orthopsychiatry,* 42 (January 1972), pp. 40-47.

Corder, B. F., et al. "An Experimental Study of the Effect of Structured Videotape Feedback on Adolescent Group Psychotherapy Process." *Journal of Youth and Adolescence,* 10 (August 1981), pp. 255-261.

Cotler, S., et al. "Evaluating a Community Mental Health Center Program for Children." *Journal of Social Service Research,* 3 (Summer 1980), pp. 361-370.

Cowen, E. L.; Gesten, E. L.; and Wilson, A. B. "The Primary Mental Health Project (PMHP): Evaluation of Current Program Effectiveness." *American Journal of Community Psychology,* 7 (June 1979), pp. 293-303.

Craig, M. M., and Fursl, P. W. "What Happens After Treatment? A

Study of Potentially Delinquent Boys." *Social Service Review,* 39 (June 1965), pp. 165-171.

Crockett, G. T. *1977 Evaluation Report.* St. Paul: Child Development Centers of Minnesota, 1977.

Csapo, M., and Agg, B. "Educational Rehabilitation of Delinquents in a Community Setting." *Canadian Journal of Criminology and Corrections,* 18 (January 1976), pp. 42-48.

D'Angelo, R. Y., and Walsh, J. F. "An Evaluation of Various Therapy Approaches with Lower Socioeconomic-Group Children." *Journal of Psychology,* 67 (January 1967), pp. 59-64.

Davids, A.; Ryan, R.; and Salvatore, P. D. "Effectiveness of Residential Treatment for Psychotic and Other Disturbed Children." *American Journal of Orthopsychiatry,* 38 (April 1968), pp. 469-475.

Davidson, W. S. II, et al. "Diversion Program for Juvenile Offenders." *Social Work Research and Abstracts,* 13 (Summer 1977), pp. 40-49.

DeLeon, C., & Mandell, W. "A Comparison of Conditioning and Psychotherapy in the Treatment of Functional Enuresis." *Journal of Clinical Psychology,* 22 (May 1966), pp. 326-330.

DiLeonardi, J. W. "Correlating Treatment Outcomes of Parents and Young Children." *Child Welfare,* 60 (April 1981), pp. 245-253.

Durlak, J. A. "Comparative Effectiveness of Behavioral and Relationship Group Treatment in the Secondary Prevention of School Maladjustment." *American Journal of Community Psychology,* 8 (June 1980), pp. 327-339.

Epstein, I., and Finch, C. "Behavior Modification in the Classroom: Education or Social Control?" *Journal of Sociology and Social Welfare,* 6 (November 1979), pp. 595-610.

Feldman, R. A. "Group Integration, Intense Interpersonal Dislike, and Social Group Work Intervention." *Social Work,* 14 (July 1969), pp. 30-39.

Feldman, R. A., and Caplinger, T. E. "Social Work Experience and Client Behavioral Change: A Multivariate Analysis of Process and Outcome." *Journal of Social Service Research,* 1 (Fall 1977), pp. 5-33.

Feldman, R. A.; Caplinger, T. E.; and Wodarski, J. S. *The St. Louis Conundrum: The Effective Treatment of Antisocial Youths.* Englewood Cliffs, N.J.: Prentice-Hall, 1983.

Fine, S.; Knight-Webb, G.; and Breau, K. "Volunteer Adolescents in Adolescent Group Therapy: Effect on Patients and Volunteers." *British Journal of Psychiatry,* 129, No. 11 (1976), pp. 407-413.

Fineberg, B. L.; Kettlewell, P. W.; and Sowards, S. K. "An Evaluation of Adolescent Inpatient Services." *American Journal of Orthopsychiatry,* 52 (April 1982), pp. 337–345.

Fleischman, M. J. "A Replication of Patterson's 'Intervention for Boys with Conduct Problems.' " *Journal of Consulting and Clinical Psychology,* 49 (June 1981), pp. 342–351.

Forgatch, M. S., and Toobetr, D. J. "A Cost-Effective Parent Training Program for Use with Normal Preschool Children." *Journal of Pediatric Psychology,* 4 (June 1979), pp. 129–145.

Ganter, G.; Yeakel, M.; and Polansky, N. A. "Intermediary Group Treatment of Inaccessible Children." *American Journal of Orthopsychiatry,* 35 (July 1965), pp. 739–746.

Garell, D. C. "A Hotline Telephone Service for Young People in Crisis." *Children,* 16 (September–October 1969), pp. 177–180.

Gittelman-Klein, R., and Klein, D. F. "Controlled Imipramine Treatment of School Phobia." *Archives of General Psychiatry,* 25 (March 1971), pp. 204–207.

Goodwin, J. *Evaluation of the Original Follow-Through Program, 1979–1980.* Philadelphia: Philadelphia School District, Office of Research and Evaluation, October 1981.

Gordon, S. B.; Lerner, L. L.; and Keefe, F. J. "Responsive Parenting: An Approach to Training Parents of Problem Children." *American Journal of Community Psychology,* 7 (February 1979), pp. 45–56.

Guzzetta, R. A. "Acquisition and Transfer of Empathy by the Parents of Early Adolescents Through Structured Learning Training." *Journal of Counseling Psychology,* 23 (October 1976), pp. 449–453.

Hamovitch, M. B. "Girls at Vocational High: An Experiment in Social Work Intervention—An Essay Review." *Child Welfare,* 44 (September–October 1965), pp. 463–465.

Hampe, E., et al. "Phobic Children: One and Two Years' Posttreatment-Follow-up." *Journal of Abnormal Psychology,* 82 (August 1973), pp. 446–453.

Handler, E. "Residential Treatment Programs for Juvenile Delinquents." *Social Work,* 20 (May 1975), pp. 217–222.

Hauserman, N.; Zweback, S.; and Plotkin, A. "Use of Concrete Reinforcement to Facilitate Verbal Initiations in Adolescent Group Therapy." *Journal of Consulting and Clinical Psychology,* 38 (February 1972), pp. 90–96.

Havelkova, M. "Follow-Up Study of 71 Children Diagnosed as Psychotic in Preschool Age." *American Journal of Orthopsychiatry,* 38 (October 1968), pp. 846-857.

Heinicke, C. M. "Aiding 'At Risk' Children Through Psychoanalytic Social Work with Parents." *American Journal of Orthopsychiatry,* 46 (January 1976), pp. 89-103.

Hill, K. T., and Stevenson, H. W. "The Effects of Social Reinforcement vs. Non-Reinforcement and Sex of E on the Performance of Adolescent Girls." *Journal of Personality,* 33 (March 1965), pp. 30-36.

Hilyer, J. C., et al. "Physical Fitness Training and Counseling as Treatment for Youthful Offenders." *Journal of Counseling Psychology,* 29 (July 1982), pp. 292-303.

Holmes, D. S., and Urie, R. G. "Effects of Preparing Children for Psychotherapy." *Journal of Consulting and Clinical Psychology,* 43 (June 1975), pp. 311-318.

Hurley, A. W. "Enhancing the Self-Concepts of High School Girls: An Exploratory Study." *School Social Work Quarterly,* 1 (Winter 1979), pp. 327-336.

Irigon, F. F., et al. "Child Development Centers Program: An Effective School-Based Mental Health Service." *Child Welfare,* 60 (September-October 1981), pp. 369-377.

Jaffe, E. D. "Effects of Institutionalization on Adolescent, Dependent Children." *Child Welfare,* 48 (February 1969), pp. 64-71 and 111.

Jayaratne, S. "Measurement of Process and Outcome in Social Practice." *Social Work in Education,* 4 (Fall 1981), pp. 30-38.

Jones, R. *Consumer and Social Worker Perceptions of Intermediate Treatment: A Low Intensity, Activity Based Group Treatment of Adolescents —Fun and Therapy.* Leicester, England: National Youth Bureau, 1979.

Kagle, J. D. "Evaluating Social Work Practice." *Social Work,* 24 (July 1979), pp. 292-296.

Karson, S. "Group Psychotherapy with Latency Age Boys." *International Journal of Group Psychotherapy,* 15, No. 1 (1965), pp. 81-89.

Kennedy, W. A. "School Phobia: Rapid Treatment of Fifty Cases." *Journal of Abnormal Psychology,* 70 (November 1965), pp. 285-289.

Kobrin, S., and Klein, M. W. *Community Treatment of Juvenile Offenders: The DSO Experiments.* Beverly Hills, Calif.: Sage Publications, 1983.

Lazarus, A. A.; Davison, G. C.; and Polefka, D. A. "Classical and Operant Factors in the Treatment of School Phobia." *Journal of Abnormal Psychology,* 70 (August 1965), pp. 225-229.

Lehrman, L. J., et al. *Success and Failure of Treatment of Children in Child Guidance Clinics of the Jewish Board of Guardians.* Research Monograph No. 1. New York: Jewish Board of Guardians, 1949.

Lessor, L. R. "A Small Agency Broadens Its Scope." *Social Casework,* 50 (March 1969), pp. 157–161.

Leventhal, T., and Weinberger, G. "Evaluation of a Large-Scale Brief Therapy Program for Children." *American Journal of Orthopsychiatry,* 45 (January 1975), pp. 119–133.

Levitt, E. "The Results of Psychotherapy with Children: An Evaluation." *Journal of Consulting Psychology,* 21 (June 1957), pp. 189–196.

Levitt, E.; Beiser, H.; and Robertson, R. "A Follow-Up Evaluation of Cases Treated at a Community Child Guidance Clinic. *American Journal of Orthopsychiatry,* 29 (March 1959), pp. 337–347.

Lindsey, E. W. "School Mental Health Programs: A Review of Evaluation Efforts." *School Social Work Quarterly,* 1 (Summer 1979), pp. 101–115.

Magary, L., and Elder, V. "Group Therapy with Adolescent Girls: Two Models." *Dynamic Approaches to Serving Families.* New York: Community Service Society, 1970, pp. 37–53.

Mann, D. *Intervening with Convicted Serious Juvenile Offenders.* Washington, D.C.: National Institute for Juvenile Justice and Delinquency Prevention, U.S. Department of Justice, 1976.

Mash, E. J.; Hardy, L. C.; and Hamerlynch, L. A., eds. *Behavior Modification and Approaches to Parenting.* New York: Brunner/Mazel, 1976.

Massimo, J. L., and Shore, M. F. "Comprehensive Vocationally Oriented Psychotherapy: A New Treatment Technique for Lower-Class Adolescent Delinquent Boys." *Psychiatry,* 30 (August 1967), pp. 229–236.

Mayadas, N. S., and Jacks, E. "Drama Groups: A Method of Promoting Inter-Cultural Understanding in Integrated Public Schools." *School Social Work Journal,* 1 (Spring 1974), pp. 51–61.

Mayers, M. O. "Results of an Experiment to Help the 'Hard Core' Delinquent for Whom Social Workers Have Difficulty in Finding a Residential Placement." *Community Home Schools Gazette,* 69, No. 7 (1975), pp. 346–352.

Mazik, K., and MacNamara, R. "Operant Conditioning at the Training School." *Training School Bulletin,* 63, No. 4 (1967), pp. 153–158.

McCarnes, K., and Smith, L. L. "Evaluating a Children's Group Treatment Program." *Social Work with Groups,* 2 (Winter 1979), pp. 343-354.

McCullagh, J. G. "Assertion Training for Boys in Junior High School." *Social Work in Education,* 5 (Fall 1982), pp. 41-51.

McKenzie, H. S., et al. "Behavior Modification of Children with Learning Disabilities Using Grades as Tokens and Allowances as Back-Up Reinforcers." *Exceptional Children,* 34, No. 10 (1968), pp. 745-752.

McMahon, R. J.; Forehand, R.; and Griest, D. L. "Effects of Knowledge of Social Learning Principles on Enhancing Treatment Outcomes and Generalization in a Parent Training Program." *Journal of Consulting and Clinical Psychology,* 49 (August 1981), pp. 526-532.

Menolascino, F. J., and Eaton, L. "Psychoses of Childhood: A Five-Year Follow-up Study of Experiences in a Mental Retardation Clinic." *American Journal of Mental Deficiency,* 73, No. 3 (1967), pp. 370-380.

Meyer, H. J.; Borgatta, E. F.; and Jones, W. C. *Girls at Vocational High: An Experiment in Social Work Intervention.* New York: Russell Sage Foundation, 1965.

Michals, A. P.; Cournoyer, D. E.; and Pinner, E. L. "School Social Work and Educational Goals." *Social Work,* 24 (April 1979), pp. 138-141.

Miller, W. B. "The Impact of a Total Community Delinquency Control Project." *Social Problems,* 10 (Fall 1962), pp. 168-191.

Millman, H. L., and Schaefer, C. E. "Behavioral Change: Program Evaluation and Staff Feedback." *Child Welfare,* 54 (December 1975), pp. 692-702.

Minde, K. K., and Werry, J. S. "Intensive Psychiatric Teacher Counseling in a Low Socioeconomic Area: A Controlled Evaluation." *American Journal of Orthopsychiatry,* 39 (July 1969), pp. 595-608.

Miskiman, D. E. "An Evaluation of a Community Outreach Program." *American Journal of Community Psychology,* 7 (February 1979), pp. 71-77.

Moadel, Y. "Adolescent Group Psychotherapy in a Hospital Setting." *American Journal of Psychoanalysis,* 30, No. 1 (1970), pp. 68-71.

Nahme-Huang, L., et al. "Imaginative Play Training and Perceptual-Motor Interventions with Emotionally-Disturbed Children." *American Journal of Orthopsychiatry,* 47 (April 1977), pp. 238-249.

Novick, J. "Symptomatic Treatment of Acquired and Persistent Enuresis." *Journal of Abnormal Psychology,* 71 (September 1966), pp. 363-368.

Ollendick, T. H., and Hersen, M. "Social Skills Training for Juvenile

Delinquents." *Behaviour Research and Therapy,* 17, No. 6 (1979), pp. 547-554.

Patterson, G. R. "Interventions for Boys with Conduct Problems: Multiple Settings, Treatments, and Criteria." *Journal of Consulting and Clinical Psychology,* 42 (August 1974), pp. 471-481.

Pearson, J. W. "A Differential Use of Group Homes for Delinquent Boys." *Children,* 17 (July-August 1970), pp. 143-148.

Persons, R. W. "Relationship Between Psychotherapy with Institutionalized Boys and Subsequent Community Adjustment." *Journal of Consulting Psychology,* 31, No. 2 (1967), pp. 137-141.

Pierson, G. R., Cattell, R. B., and Pierce, J. "A Demonstration by the HSPQ of the Nature of the Personality Changes Produced by Institutionalization of Delinquents." *Journal of Social Psychology,* 70 (1966), pp. 229-239.

Pinkston, E. M., and Herbert-Jackson, E. W. "Modification of Irrelevant and Bizarre Verbal Behavior Using Parents as Therapists." *Social Service Review,* 49 (March 1975), pp. 46-63.

Pisapia, M. L., and Hanwell, A. F. "Social Work in Day Care." *Child Welfare,* 48 (May 1969), pp. 268-272 and 278.

Pollack, D. "A Sensitivity-Training Approach to Group Therapy with Children." *Child Welfare,* 50 (February 1971), pp. 86-89.

Polster, R. A., and Pinkston, E. M. "A Delivery System for the Treatment of Underachievement." *Social Service Review,* 53 (March 1979), pp. 35-55.

Powers, E., and Witmer, H. *An Experiment in the Prevention of Delinquency—The Cambridge-Somerville Youth Study.* New York: Columbia University Press, 1951.

Radin, N. "Assessing the Effectiveness of School Social Workers." *Social Work,* 24 (March 1979), pp. 132-137.

Reid, W. J., et al. "Task-Centered School Social Work." *Social Work in Education,* 2 (Winter 1980), pp. 7-24.

Reker, G. T.; Cote, J. E.; and Peacock, E. J. "Juvenile Diversion: Conceptual Issues and Program Effectiveness." *Canadian Journal of Criminology,* 22 (January 1980), pp. 36-50.

Rose, S. D. "Group Training of Parents as Behavior Modifiers." *Social Work,* 19 (March 1974), pp. 156-162.

Rosenstock, H. A., and Vincent, K. R. "Parental Involvement as a Requisite for Successful Adolescent Therapy." *Journal of Clinical Psychiatry,* 40, No. 3 (1979), pp. 132-134.

Rubenstein, J. S., et al. "The Parent-Therapist Program: Alternate Care for Emotionally Disturbed Children." *American Journal of Orthopsychiatry,* 48 (October 1978), pp. 654-661.

Schaffer, E. B. "A New Approach to Delinquency Prevention—The Illinois Policy/Social Service Project." *Police Journal,* 49 (January 1976), pp. 35-41.

Schinke, S. P. "School-Based Model for Preventing Teenage Pregnancy." *Social Work in Education,* 4 (Winter 1982), pp. 34-42.

Schinke, S. P., et al. "Primary Prevention of Adolescent Pregnancy." *Social Work With Groups,* 4, Nos. 1-2 (1981), pp. 121-135.

Schinke, S. P.; Blythe, B. J.; and Gilchrist, L. D. "Cognitive-Behavioral Prevention of Adolescent Pregnancy." *Journal of Counseling Psychology,* 28, No. 5 (1981), pp. 451-454.

Schinke, S. P., and Gilchrist, L. D. "Adolescent Pregnancy: An Interpersonal Skill Training Approach to Prevention." *Social Work in Health Care,* 3 (Spring 1977), pp. 159-167.

Schofield, R. "Parent Group Education and Student Self-Esteem." *Social Work in Education,* 1 (January 1979), pp. 26-33.

Schwitzgebel, R. L. "Short-term Operant Conditioning of Adolescent Offenders on Socially Relevant Variables." *Journal of Abnormal Psychology,* 72 (May 1967), pp. 134-142.

Scott, T. J. "The Use of Music to Reduce Hyperactivity in Children." *American Journal of Orthopsychiatry,* 40 (July 1970), pp. 677-680.

Seidel, H. E., Jr., Barkley, M. J., and Stith, D. "Evaluation of a Program for Project Head Start." *Journal of Genetic Psychology,* 110 (1967), pp. 185-197.

Shone, N., and Christie, R. "Police, Social Workers and Children in Trouble—A Study in Liaison." *Journal of Social Welfare Law,* 3 (1979), pp. 147-154.

Shore, M. F., and Massimo, J. L. "Comprehensive Vocationally Oriented Psychotherapy for Adolescent Delinquent Boys: A Follow-up Study." *American Journal of Orthopsychiatry,* 36 (July 1966), pp. 609-615.

———. "Five Years Later: A Follow-up Study of Comprehensive Vocationally Oriented Psychotherapy." *American Journal of Orthopsychiatry,* 39 (October 1969), pp. 769-773.

Signell, K. A. "Kindergarten Entry: A Preventive Approach to Community Mental Health." *Community Mental Health Journal,* 8, No. 1 (1972), pp. 60-70.

Silverman, M. A., and Wolfson, E. "Early Intervention and Social Class." *Journal of the American Academy of Child Psychiatry,* 10 (December 1971), pp. 603-618.

Spence, S. H., and Marzillier, J. S. "Social Skills Training with Adolescent Male Offenders—II. Short-Term, Long-Term and Generalized Effects." *Behaviour Research and Therapy,* 19, No. 4 (1981), pp. 349-368.

Sprince, M. P., and Baker, S. "Work with Adolescents: Brief Psychotherapy with a Limited Aim." *Journal of Child Psychotherapy,* 2, No. 2 (1968), pp. 31-37.

Swerdlik, M.; Rice, W.; and Larson, E. "The Effect of a Group Therapy Experience on Fifth Grade Acting Out Boys." *School Social Work Journal,* 2 (Spring 1978), pp. 83-88.

Taber, S. M. "Cognitive-Behavior Modification Treatment of an Aggressive 11-Year-Old Boy." *Social Work Research and Abstracts,* 17 (Summer 1981), pp. 13-23.

Tait, C., and Hodges, E. *Delinquents, Their Families and the Community.* Springfield, Ill.: Charles C Thomas, 1962.

Taylor, A. J. W. "An Evaluation of Group Psychotherapy in a Girl's Borstal." *International Journal of Group Psychotherapy,* 17, No. 2 (1967), pp. 168-177.

Taylor, D. F., and Albert, S. W. *Community and Support Following Residential Treatment.* New York: Child Welfare League of America, 1973.

Taylor, J. G., et al. *A Group Home for Adolescent Girls—Practice and Research.* New York: Child Welfare League of America, 1976.

Therrien, M. E. "Evaluating Empathy Skill Training for Parents." *Social Work,* 24 (September 1979), pp. 417-419.

Thoma, E. "Group Psychotherapy with Underachieving Girls in a Public High School." *Journal of Individual Psychology,* 20, No. 1 (1964), pp. 96-100.

Tobiessen, J., and Shai, A. "A Comparison of Individual and Group Mental Health Consultation with Teachers." *Community Mental Health Journal,* 7, No. 3 (1971), pp. 218-226.

Tolson, E. R., and Brown, L. B. "Client Dropout Rate and Students' Practice Skills in Task-Centered Casework." *Social Casework: The Journal of Contemporary Social Work,* 62 (May 1981), pp. 308-313.

Truax, C. B., et al. "Effects of Therapeutic Conditions in Child Therapy." *Journal of Community Psychology,* 1 (June-July 1973), pp. 313-318.

Truax, C. B.; Wargo, D. G.; and Volksdorf, N. R. "Antecedents to Outcome in Group Counseling with Institutionalized Juvenile Delinquents: Effects of Therapeutic Conditions, Patient Self-Exploration, Alternate Sessions, and Vicarious Pretraining." *Journal of Abnormal Psychology,* 76 (May 1970), pp. 235-242.

Tyler, V. O., Jr., and Brown, G. D. "The Use of Swift, Brief Isolation as a Group Control Device for Institutionalized Delinquents." *Behaviour Research and Therapy,* 5, No. 1 (1967), pp. 1-9.

Wahler, R. G., and Erickson, M. "Child Behavior Therapy: A Community Program in Appalachia." *Behaviour Research and Therapy,* 7, No. 1 (1969), pp. 71-78.

Waterhouse, J. "Group Work in Intermediate Treatment." *British Journal of Social Work,* 8, No. 2 (1978), pp. 127-144.

Webb, A. P., and Riley, P. "Effectiveness of Casework with Young Female Probationers." *Social Casework,* 51 (November 1970), pp. 566-573.

Wilgosh, L. "A Study of Group Home Placements as a Possible Correction of Delinquent Behaviour." *Canadian Journal of Criminology and Corrections,* 15 (January 1973), pp. 100-108.

Wittes, G., and Radin, N. "Two Approaches to Group Work with Parents in a Compensatory Preschool Program." *Social Work,* 16 (January 1971), pp. 42-50.

Wodarski, J. S.; Rubeiz, G. M.; and Feldman, R. A. "Program Planning for Antisocial Boys." *Social Work,* 19 (November 1974), pp. 705-713.

Wolf, J. G., and Sylves, D. *Niagara County Comprehensive Planning Evaluation Project: Year One Report.* Albany: New York State Division of Youth, 1979.

Wolins, M. "Group Care: Friend or Foe?" *Social Work,* 14 (January 1969), pp. 35-53.

Wolins, M.; Wozner, Y.; and Shye, S. "Rejuvenating the Asylum: A Field Study." *Social Work Research and Abstracts,* 16 (Spring 1980), pp. 17-25.

Zastrow, C. H. "The Nominal Group: A New Approach to Designing Programs for Curbing Delinquency." *Canadian Journal of Criminology and Corrections,* 15 (January 1973), pp. 109-120.

Zastrow, C. H., and Navarre, R. "Help for Runaways and Their Parents." *Social Casework,* 56 (February 1975), pp. 74-78.

Zeff, S. B. "Program for Disadvantaged Elementary School Students." *Social Work in Education,* 4 (Fall 1981), pp. 19-29.

Community Intervention

Datta, L. E. "Head Start's Influence on Community Change." *Children,* 17 (September–October 1970), pp. 193–196.

Kamerman, S. B. "Participation, Leadership, and Expertise: Imbalance or in Balance?" *Social Service Review,* 48 (September 1974), pp. 403–411.

Lyden, F. J., and Lee, L. K. "Evaluating Program Change." *Social Work,* 18 (March 1973), pp. 87–94.

Spiro, S. E. "Ex post facto Evaluation of Neighborhood Organization Programs." *Journal of Sociology and Social Welfare,* 4 (September 1977), pp. 783–795.

Corrections

Agopian, M. W. "Evaluation of Adult Diversion Programs: The California Experience." *Federal Probation,* 41, No. 3 (1977), pp. 15–18.

Barnett, O. "Nonprofessionals in the Rehabilitation of Mentally Disordered Sex Offenders." *Community Mental Health Journal,* 14, No. 2 (1978), pp. 110–115.

Heinz, J.; Galaway, B.; and Hudson, J. "Restitution or Parole: A Follow-Up Study of Adult Offenders." *Social Service Review,* 50 (March 1976), pp. 148–156.

Hood, R. "Social Work in Prison." *British Journal of Criminology,* 15, No. 3 (1975), pp. 277–280.

Kirby, B. C. "Crofton House: An Experiment with a County Halfway House." *Federal Probation,* 33, No. 1 (1969), pp. 53–58.

Leak, G. K. "Effects of Highly Structured Versus Nondirective Group Counseling Approaches on Personality and Behavioral Measures of Adjustment in Incarcerated Felons." *Journal of Counseling Psychology,* 27 (October 1980), pp. 520–523.

Lichtman, C. M., and Smock, S. M. "The Effects of Social Services on Probationer Recidivism: A Field Experiment." *Journal of Research in Crime and Delinquency,* 18 (February 1981), pp. 81–100.

Scharf, P.; Hickey, J. E.; and Moriarty, T. "Moral Conflict and Change in Correctional Settings." *Personnel and Guidance Journal,* 51 (May 1973), pp. 660–663.

Schauss, A. G. "Differential Outcomes among Probationers Comparing Orthomolecular Approaches to Conventional Casework/Counseling." *Journal of Orthomolecular Psychiatry,* 8, No. 3 (1979), pp. 158–168.

Sinclair, I. A. C.; Shaw, M. J.; and Troop, J. "The Relationship Between

Introversion and Response to Casework in a Prison Setting." *British Journal of Social and Clinical Psychology,* 13, No. 1 (1974), pp. 51-60.

Developmental Disabilities

Andrews, R. J., and Berry, P. B. "The Evaluation of Services for the Handicapped Promoting Community Living." *International Journal of Rehabilitation Research,* 1 (October 1978), pp. 451-461.

Baker, B. L., and Ward, M. H. "Reinforcement Therapy for Behavior Problems in Severely Retarded Children." *American Journal of Orthopsychiatry,* 41 (January 1971), pp. 124-135.

Berkson, G. "Social Ecology of Supervised Communal Facilities for Mentally Disabled Adults: V. Residence as a Predictor of Social and Work Adjustment." *American Journal of Mental Deficiency,* 86, No. 1 (1981), pp. 39-42.

Birenbaum, A., and Re, M. A. "Resettling Mentally Retarded Adults in the Community—Almost Four Years Later." *American Journal of Mental Deficiency,* 84, No. 4 (1979), pp. 323-329.

Bradley, B. H.; Maurer, R.; and Hundziak, M. "A Study of the Effectiveness of Milieu Therapy and Language Training for the Mentally Retarded." *Exceptional Children,* 33 (November 1966), pp. 143-150.

Bruininks, R. H.; Hill, B. K.; and Thorsheim, M. J. "Deinstitutionalization and Foster Care for Mentally Retarded People." *Health and Social Work,* 7 (August 1982), pp. 198-205.

Campbell, D. R., and Browning, P. L. "Therapists' Approach and Avoidance Responses and the Verbal Behavior of Mentally Retarded Clients." *Journal of Counseling Psychology,* 22 (August 1975), pp. 320-323.

Cogan, F.; Monson, L.; and Bruggeman, W. "Concurrent Group and Individual Treatment of the Mentally Retarded." *Corrective Psychiatry and Journal of Social Therapy,* 12, No. 5 (1966), pp. 404-409.

Doubros, S. G. "An Investigation of Verbal Conditioning in Level II Adolescent Retardates." *American Journal of Mental Deficiency,* 71, No. 5 (1967), pp. 806-810.

Dykman, R. A., et al. "Children with Learning Disabilities: Conditioning, Differentiation, and the Effect of Distraction." *American Journal of Orthopsychiatry,* 40 (October 1970), pp. 766-782.

Giles, D. K., and Wolf, M. M. "Toilet Training Institutionalized, Severe Retardates: An Application of Operant Behavior Modification Techniques." *American Journal of Mental Deficiency,* 70, No. 5 (1966), pp. 766-780.

Goldin, G. J.; Margolin, R. J.; and Stotsky, B. A. "Motivational Factors in the Rehabilitation Facility." *Rehabilitation Literature,* 29 (June 1968), pp. 66-72.

Grinnell, R. M., Jr., and Lieberman, A. "Teaching the Mentally Retarded Job Interviewing Skills." *Journal of Counseling Psychology,* 24 (August 1977), pp. 332-337.

Halpern, A. S. "The Impact of Work Study Programs on Employment of the Mentally Retarded: Some Findings from Sources." *International Journal of Rehabilitation Research,* 1 (April 1978), pp. 167-175.

Heinicke, C. M. "Frequency of Psychotherapeutic Sessions as a Factor Affecting Outcome: Analysis of Clinical Ratings and Test Results." *Journal of Abnormal Psychology,* 74 (1969), pp. 553-560.

Kurtz, P. D. "Using Mass Media and Group Instruction for Preventive Mental Health in Rural Communities." *Social Work Research and Abstracts,* 18 (Fall 1982), pp. 41-48.

Lee, D. Y. "Evaluation of a Group Counseling Program Designed to Enhance Social Adjustment of Mentally Retarded Adults." *Journal of Counseling Psychology,* 24 (August 1977), pp. 318-323.

Litrownik, J. L.; Freitas, J. L.; and Franzini, L. R. "Self-Regulation in Mentally Retarded Children: Assessment and Training of Self-Monitoring Skills." *American Journal of Mental Deficiency,* 82, No. 5 (1978), pp. 499-506.

Mann, P. H.; Beaber, J. D.; and Jacobson, M. D. "The Effect of Group Counseling on Educable Mentally Retarded Boys' Self-Concepts." *Exceptional Children,* 35 (February 1969), pp. 359-366.

Matson, J. L. "A Controlled Outcome Study of Phobias in Mentally Retarded Adults." *Behaviour Research and Therapy,* 19, No. 2 (1981), pp. 101-107.

Matson, J. L., and Senator, V. "A Comparison of Traditional Psychotherapy and Social Skills Training for Improving Interpersonal Functioning of Mentally Retarded Adults." *Behavior Therapy,* 12 (1981), pp. 369-382.

Meyer, R. J. "Patterns of Family Follow-up: A Study of Children with Mental Retardation and Associated Developmental Disorders." *Community Mental Health Journal,* 6, No. 5 (1970), pp. 393-400.

Miezio, S. "Group Therapy with Mentally Retarded Adolescents in Institutional Settings." *International Journal of Group Psychotherapy,* 17 (July 1967), pp. 321-327.

Morrison, D., and Pothier, P. "Effects of Sensory-Motor Training on the Language Development of Retarded Preschoolers." *American Journal of Orthopsychiatry,* 48 (April 1978), pp. 310–319.

Mueller, B. J., and Porter, R. "Placement of Adult Retardates from State Institutions in Community Care Facilities." *Community Mental Health Journal,* 5, No. 4 (1969), pp. 289–294.

Philipp, C., and Siefert, K. "A Study of Maternal Participation in Preschool Programs for Handicapped Children and Their Families." *Social Work in Health Care,* 5 (Winter 1979), pp. 165–175.

Pumphrey, M. W.; Goodman, M.; and Flax, N. "Integrating Individuals with Impaired Adaptive Behavior in a Group Work Agency." In *Social Work Practice, 1969.* New York: Columbia University Press, 1969.

Rubin, J. *Alternatives in Rehabilitating the Handicapped: A Policy Analysis.* New York: Human Sciences Press, 1982.

Santostefano, S., and Stayton, S. "Training the Preschool Retarded Child in Focusing Attention: A Program for Parents." *American Journal of Orthopsychiatry,* 37 (July 1967), pp. 732–743.

Schrader, C.; Shaull, J.; and Elmore, B. "Behavioral Treatment of Self-Stimulation in the Developmentally Disabled." *Behavior Modification,* 7 (April 1983), pp. 267–294.

Senatore, V.; Matson, J. L.; and Kazdin, A. E. "A Comparison of Behavioral Methods to Train Social Skills to Mentally Retarded Adults." *Behavior Therapy,* 13, No. 3 (1982), pp. 313–324.

Sessoms, H. D. "Organized Camping and the Handicapped Child: A Three-Year Study." *Rehabilitation Literature,* 40 (April 1979), pp. 40–43.

Stacy, D.; Doleys, D. M.; and Malcolm, R. "Effects of Social-Skills Training in a Community-Based Program." *Journal of Mental Deficiency,* 84, No., 2 (1979), pp. 152–158.

Stone, N. D., and Parnicky, J. J. "Factors in Child Placement: Parental Response to Congenital Defect." *Social Work,* 11 (April 1966), pp. 35–43.

Tarran, E. C. "Parents' Views of Medical and Social Work Services for Families with Young Cerebral-Palsied Children." *Developmental Medicine and Child Neurology,* 23, No. 2 (1981), pp. 173–182.

Tavormina, J. B.; Hampson, R. B.; and Luscomb, R. L. "Participant Evaluations of the Effectiveness of Their Parent Counseling Groups." *Mental Retardation,* 14 (December 1976), pp. 8–9.

Family Treatment

Alexander, J. F., and Parsons, B. V. "Short-term Behavioral Intervention with Delinquent Families: Impact on Family Process and Recidivism." *Journal of Abnormal Psychology,* 81 (August 1973), pp. 219–225.

Alkire, A. A., and Brunse, A. J. "Impact and Possible Casualty from Videotape Feedback in Marital Therapy." *Journal of Consulting and Clinical Psychology,* 42 (April 1974), pp. 203–210.

Bader, E., "Do Marriage Preparation Programs Really Work? A Canadian Experiment." *Journal of Marital and Family Therapy,* 6 (April 1980).

Bellville, T. P.; Raths, O. N.; and Bellville, C. J. "Conjoint Marriage Therapy with a Husband-and-Wife Team." *American Journal of Orthopsychiatry,* 39 (April 1969), pp. 473–483.

Besalel, V. A., and Azrin, N. H. "The Reduction of Parent-Youth Problems by Reciprocity Counseling." *Behaviour Research and Therapy,* 19, No. 4 (1981), pp. 297–301.

Blechman, E. A., et al. "Engagement in Behavioral Family Therapy: A Multisite Investigation." *Behavior Therapy,* 12, No. 4 (1981), pp. 461–472.

Brandreth, A., and Pike, R. "Assessment of Marriage Counseling in a Small Family Agency." *Social Work,* 12 (October 1967), pp. 34–39.

Braxton, D. "Family Casework and Juvenile First Offenders." *Social Casework,* 47 (February 1966), pp. 87–92.

Brown, J. S. "Family Life Education for High-risk Young Families." In *Social Work Practice, 1967.* New York: Columbia University Press, 1967, pp. 165–177.

Carkhuff, R. R., and Bierman, R. "Training as a Preferred Mode of Treatment of Parents of Emotionally Disturbed Children." *Journal of Counseling Psychology,* 17 (April 1970), pp. 157–161.

Christensen, A., et al. "Cost Effectiveness in Behavioral Family Therapy." *Behavior Therapy,* 11, No. 2 (1980), pp. 208–226.

Coughlin, F., and Wimberger, H. C. "Group Family Therapy." *Family Process,* 7 (March 1968), pp. 37–50.

Dalton, P. "Family Treatment of an Obsessive-Compulsive Child: A Case Report." *Family Process,* 22 (March 1983), pp. 99–108.

Davis, L. V., and Carlson, B. E. "Attitudes of Service Providers Toward Domestic Violence." *Social Work Research and Abstracts,* 17 (Winter 1981), pp. 34–39.

Edelson, R. I., and Seidman, E. "Use of Videotaped Feedback in Altering Interpersonal Perceptions of Married Couples: A Therapy Analogue."

Journal of Consulting and Clinical Psychology, 43 (April 1975), pp. 244-250.

Falloon, I. R. H., et al. "Family Therapy of Schizophrenics with High Risk of Relapse." *Family Process,* 20 (June 1981), pp. 211-221.

Fischer, J., et al. "Adlerian Family Counseling: An Evaluation." *American Journal of Family Therapy,* 6 (Summer 1978), pp. 42-44.

Fisher, S. G. "The Use of Time Limits in Brief Psychotherapy: A Comparison of Six-Session, Twelve-Session, and Unlimited Treatment with Families." *Family Process,* 19 (December 1980), pp. 377-392.

Forehand, R., et al. "Side Effects of Parent Counseling on Marital Satisfaction." *Journal of Counseling Psychology,* 29 (January 1982), pp. 104-107.

Frank, E.; Anderson, C.; and Rubinstein, D. "Marital Role Ideals and Perception of Marital Role Behavior in Distressed and Non-Distressed Couples." *Journal of Marital and Family Therapy,* 6 (January 1980), pp. 55-63.

Gerreira, A. J., and Winter, W. D. "Stability of Interactional Variables in Family Decision-making." *Archives of General Psychiatry,* 14 (April 1966), pp. 352-355.

Golner, J. H. "Home Family Counseling." *Social Work,* 16 (October 1971), pp. 63-71.

Gurman, A. S. "Couples' Facilitative Communication Skill as a Dimension of Marital Therapy Outcome." *Journal of Marriage and Family Counseling,* 1, No. 2 (1975), pp. 163-174.

Hollis, F. "Continuance and Discontinuance in Marital Counseling and Some Observations on Joint Interviews." *Social Casework,* 49 (March 1968), pp. 167-174.

Jayaratne, S. "Behavioral Intervention and Family Decision-Making." *Social Work,* 23 (January 1978), pp. 20-25.

Kadis, L. B., and McClendon, R. A. "Redecision Family Therapy: Its Use with Intensive Multiple Family Groups." *American Journal of Family Therapy,* 9 (Summer 1981), pp. 75-83.

Kinney, J. M., et al. "Homebuilders: Keeping Families Together." *Journal of Consulting and Clinical Psychology,* 45 (August 1977), pp. 667-673.

Krill, D. F. "Family Interviewing as an Intake Diagnostic Method." *Social Work,* 13 (April 1968), pp. 56-63.

Langsley, D. G.; Flomenhaft, K.; and Machotka, P. "Follow-Up Evaluation of Family Crisis Therapy." *American Journal of Orthopsychiatry,* 39 (October 1969), pp. 753-759.

LeCroy, C. W.; Koeplin-LeCroy, M. T.; and Long, J. "Preventive Intervention Through Parent-Training Programs." *Social Work in Education,* 4 (Winter 1982), pp. 53–62.

Liberman, R. P.; Wheeler, E.; and Sanders, N. "Behavioral Therapy for Marital Disharmony: An Educational Approach." *Journal of Marriage and Family Counseling,* 2 (1976), pp. 383–395.

Mabley, A. "Group Application Interviews in a Family Agency." *Social Casework,* 47 (March 1966), pp. 158–164.

Meddin, J., and Wattenberg, S. H. "Students and Short-Term Family Therapy: An Assessment." *Social Casework: The Journal of Contemporary Social Work,* 63 (April 1982), pp. 195–202.

Most, E. "Measuring Change in Marital Satisfaction." *Social Work,* 9 (July 1964), pp. 64–70.

"Multiple Family Therapy of Mental Patients." Unpublished report of the Research Foundation for Mental Hygiene, November 1971. Available through National Technical Information Service, Access No. PB-216-4291.

O'Leary, K. D., and Turkewitz, H. "A Comparative Outcome Study of Behavioral Marital Therapy and Communication Therapy." *Journal of Marital and Family Therapy,* 7 (April 1981), pp. 159–169.

Osofsky, H. J., and Osofsky, J. D. "Adolescents as Mothers: Results of a Program for Low-income Pregnant Teenagers with Some Emphasis upon Infants' Development." *American Journal of Orthopsychiatry,* 40 (October 1970), pp. 825–834.

Reiss, D., et al. "The Family Meets the Hospital: A Laboratory Forecast of the Encounter." *Archives of General Psychiatry,* 37 (February 1980), pp. 141–154.

Rice, C. G.; Fey, W. F.; and Kepecs, J. G. "Therapist Experience and 'Style' as Factors in Co-Therapy." *Family Process,* 11 (March 1972), pp. 1–12.

Ridley, C. A., et al. "The Effects of Relationship Enhancement and Problem-Solving Programs on Perceived Heterosexual Competence." *Family Therapy,* 8, No. 2 (1981), pp. 59–66.

Ritterman, M. K. "Hemophilia in Context: Adjunctive Hypnosis for Families with a Hemophiliac Member." *Family Process,* 21 (December 1982), pp. 469–476.

Rosenberg, B. N., and Klein, J. M. "A Family Agency Integrates Planned Short-Term Treatment." *Social Casework: The Journal of Contemporary Social Work,* 61 (December 1980), pp. 619–628.

Ro-Trock, K. G., Wellisch, D. K., and Schoolar, J. C. "A Family Therapy

Outcome Study in an Inpatient Setting." *American Journal of Orthopsychiatry,* 47 (July 1977), pp. 514-522.

Safer, D. J. "Family Therapy for Children with Behavior Disorders." *Family Process,* 5 (June 1966), pp. 243-255.

Schreiber, L. E. "Evaluation of Family Group Treatment in a Family Agency." *Family Process,* 5 (March 1966), pp. 21-29.

Shapiro, R. J., and Budman, S. H. "Defection, Termination, and Continuation in Family and Individual Therapy." *Family Process,* 12 (March 1973), pp. 55-67.

Slavson, S. R. "Coordinated Family Therapy." *International Journal of Group Psychotherapy,* 15, No. 2 (1965), pp. 177-186.

Slipp, S.; Ellis, S.; and Kressel, K. "Factors Associated with Engagement in Family Therapy." *Family Process,* 13 (December 1974), pp. 413-427.

Valle, S. K., and Marinelli, R. P. "Training in Human Relations Skills as a Preferred Mode of Treatment for Married Couples." *Journal of Marriage and Family Counseling,* 1, No. 4 (1975), pp. 359-365.

Wattie, B. "Evaluating Short-term Casework in a Family Agency." *Social Casework,* 54 (December 1973), pp. 609-616.

Wells, R. A.; Figurel, J. A.; and McNamee, P. "Communications Training vs. Conjoint Marital Therapy." *Social Work Research and Abstracts,* 13 (Summer 1977), pp. 31-39.

Woodward, C. A., et al. "Client, Treatment, and Therapist Variables Related to Outcome in Brief, System-Oriented Family Therapy." *Family Process,* 20 (June 1981), pp. 189-197.

Woodward, C. A., et al. "The Role of Goal Attainment Scaling in Evaluating Family Therapy Outcome." *American Journal of Orthopsychiatry,* 48 (July 1978), pp. 464-476.

Wright, M. K. "Comprehensive Services for Adolescent Unwed Mothers." *Children,* 13 (September-October 1966), pp. 171-176.

Gerontology

Abrahams, J. P.; Wallach, H. F.; and Divens, S. "Behavioral Improvements in Long-Term Geriatric Patients During an Age-Integrated Psychosocial Rehabilitation Program." *Journal of the American Geriatrics Society,* 27 (May 1979), pp. 218-221.

Adams, R. A. "Protective Services for the Aged." Unpublished report, 1973. Available through National Technical Information Service, Access No. SHR 0000649.

Berger, R., and Piliavin, I. "The Effect of Casework: A Research Note." *Social Work,* 21 (May 1976), pp. 205-208.

Berkman, B., and Clark, E. "Social Work's Contribution to Care of Elderly Patients: An Accountability Approach." *The Gerontologist,* 15 (October 1975), p. 93.

Berkman, B., and Rehr, H. "Elderly Patients and Their Families: Factors Related to Satisfaction with Hospital Social Services." *The Gerontologist,* 15 (December 1975), pp. 524-528.

Blackman, D. K.; Gehle, C.; and Pinkston, E. M. "Modifying Eating Habits of the Institutional Elderly." *Social Work Research and Abstracts,* 15 (Fall 1979), pp. 18-24.

Blenkner, M.; Bloom, M.; and Nielsen, M. "A Research and Demonstration Project of Protective Services." *Social Casework,* 52 (September-October 1971), pp. 483-499.

Blenkner, M., et al. *Protective Services for Older People: Findings from the Benjamin Rose Institute Study.* Cleveland, Ohio: Benjamin Rose Institute, 1974.

Blenkner, M.; Jahn, J.; and Wasser, E. *Serving the Aging: An Experiment in Social Work and Public Health Nursing.* New York: Community Service Society, 1964.

Bourestom, N., and Tars, S. "Alterations in Life Patterns Following Nursing Home Relocation." *The Gerontologist,* 14 (December 1974), pp. 506-510.

Breslau, N., and Haug, M. R. "The Elderly Aid the Elderly: The Senior Friends Program." *Social Security Bulletin,* 35 (November 1972), pp. 9-15.

Cornbleth, T. "Evaluation of Goal Attainment in Geriatric Settings." *Journal of the American Geriatrics Society,* 26 (September 1978), pp. 404-407.

Cotter, P., and Davidson, W. B. "Influence of Social Services on Well-Being Among the Aged." *Evaluation and Program Planning,* 1, No. 2 (1978), pp. 159-160.

Evans, R. L., and Jaureguy, B. M. "Group Therapy by Phone: A Cognitive Behavioral Program for Visually Impaired Elderly." *Social Work in Health Care,* 7 (Spring 1981), pp. 79-89.

Gerontological Society Committee on Research and Development. *Evaluative Research on Social Programs for the Elderly: Report of a Seminar: Portland, Oregon, June 1973 and Miami, Florida, November 1973.* Washington, D.C.: U.S. Government Printing Office, 1977.

Glamser, F. D., and DeJong, G. F. "The Efficacy of Preretirement Preparation Programs for Industrial Workers." *Journal of Gerontology,* 30 (September 1975), pp. 595–600.

Goldberg, E. M.; Mortimer, A.; and Williams, B. T. *Helping the Aged: A Field Experiment in Social Work.* London, England: George Allen & Unwin, 1970.

Harris, J. E., and Bodden, J. L. "An Activity Group Experience for Disengaged Elderly Persons." *Journal of Counseling Psychology,* 25 (August 1978), pp. 325–330.

Hiltz, S. R. "Evaluating a Pilot Social Service Project for Widows: A Chronicle of Research Problems." *Journal of Sociology and Social Welfare,* 1 (June 1974), pp. 217–224.

Hughston, G. A., and Merriam, S. B. "Reminiscence: A Nonformal Technique for Improving Cognitive Functioning in the Aged." *International Journal of Aging and Human Development,* 15, No. 2 (1982), pp. 139–149.

Hwalek, M. "Intervention with the Elderly in Information and Referral Agencies." *Social Work,* 26 (May 1981), pp. 217–221.

Katz, M. M. "Behavioral Change in the Chronicity Pattern of Dementia in the Institutional Geriatric Resident." *Journal of the American Geriatrics Society,* 24 (November 1976), pp. 522–528.

Keith, P. M. "Evaluation of Services for the Aged by Professionals and the Elderly." *Social Service Review,* 49 (June 1975), pp. 271–278.

Keller, J. F.; Croake, J. W.; and Brooking, J. Y. "Effects of a Program in Rational Thinking on Anxieties in Older Persons." *Journal of Counseling Psychology,* 22 (February 1975), pp. 54–57.

Killian, E. C. "Effect of Geriatric Transfers on Mortality Rates." *Social Work,* 15 (January 1970), pp. 19–26.

LaVorgna, D. "Group Treatment for Wives of Patients with Alzheimer's Disease." *Social Work and Health Care,* 5 (Spring 1979), pp. 219–221.

Lazarus, L. W., et al. "A Pilot Study of an Alzheimer Patients' Relatives Discussion Group." *The Gerontologist,* 21 (August 1981), pp. 353–358.

Leviton, D., and Santa Maria, L. "The Adults Health and Developmental Program: Descriptive and Evaluative Data." *The Gerontologist,* 19 (December 1979), pp. 534–543.

Liederman, P. C.; Green, R.; and Liederman, V. R. "Outpatient Group Therapy with Geriatric Patients." *Geriatrics,* 22 (January 1967), pp. 148–153.

Linsk, N.; Howe, M. W.; and Pinkston, E. M. "Behavioral Group Work in a Home for the Aged." *Social Work,* 20 (November 1975), pp. 454–463.

Matefy, R. E. "Evaluation of a Remediation Program Using Senior Citizens as Psychoeducational Agents." *Community Mental Health Journal,* 14, No. 4 (1978), pp. 327–336.

Mercer, S., and Kane, R. A. "Helplessness and Hopelessness Among the Institutionalized Aged: An Experiment." *Health and Social Work,* 4 (February 1979), pp. 90–116.

Mercer, S. O., and Garner, J. D. "Social Work Consultation in Long-Term Care Facilities." *Health and Social Work,* 6 (May 1981), pp. 5–13.

Mishara, B. L., and Kastenbaum, R. "Wine in the Treatment of Long-Term Geriatric Patients in Mental Institutions." *Journal of the American Geriatrics Society,* 22 (February 1974), pp. 88–94.

Mueller, D. J., and Atlas, L. "Resocialization of Regressed Elderly Residents: A Behavioral Management Approach." *Journal of Gerontology,* 27 (May 1972), pp. 390–392.

Nigl, A., and Jackson, B. "A Behavior Management Program to Increase Social Responses in Psychogeriatric Patients." *Journal of the American Geriatrics Society,* 29 (February 1981), pp. 92–95.

Ogren, E. H., and Linn, M. "Male Nursing Home Patients: Relocation and Mortality." *Journal of the American Geriatrics Society,* 19 (March 1971), pp. 229–239.

Ronch, J. L., and Maizler, J. S. "Individual Psychotherapy with the Institutionalized Aged." *American Journal of Orthopsychiatry,* 47 (April 1977), pp. 275–283.

Sheppard, N. A., and Valla, D. C. "Project V-Strap: An Evaluative Study of Workshops Training the Aged for Community Service." *The Gerontologist,* 16 (August 1976), pp. 356–362.

Silverstein, S. "A New Venture in Group Work with the Aged." *Social Casework,* 50 (December 1969), pp. 573–580.

State of Florida Project In-Step. *An Environment of Opportunity for Older Americans: Final Report.* Tallahassee: Florida Department of Health and Rehabilitative Services, 1975.

Stein, S. R.; Linn, M. W.; and Weiner, A. S. "Effectiveness of a Service Workers' Action Team (SWAT) for the Elderly." *Journal of the American Geriatrics Society,* 29 (September 1981), pp. 411–417.

Tarpy, K. K.; O'Donnell, T.; and Glynn, J. F. "Intensive Casework with Chronically Ill, Neuro-Psychiatric Geriatric Patients." *Journal of the American Geriatrics Society,* 12 (November 1964), pp. 1077–1082.

Toseland, R. W., Decker, J.; and Bliesner, J. A. "A Community Outreach Program for Socially Isolated Older Persons." *Journal of Gerontological Social Work,* 1 (Spring 1979), pp. 211–224.

Toseland, R. W., and Rose, S. D. "Evaluating Social Skills Training for Older Adults in Groups." *Social Work Research and Abstracts,* 14 (Spring 1978), pp. 28–33.

Toseland, R. W.; Sherman, E.; and Bliven, S. "The Comparative Effectiveness of Two Group Work Approaches for the Development of Mutual Support Groups Among the Elderly." *Social Work with Groups,* 4, Nos. 1–2 (1981), pp. 137–153.

Turbow, S. R. "Geriatric Group Day Care and Its Effect on Independent Living: A Thirty-Six Month Assessment." *The Gerontologist,* 15 (December 1975), pp. 508–515.

Vachon, M. L. S., et al. "A Controlled Study of Self-Help Intervention for Widows." *American Journal of Psychiatry,* 137 (November 1980), pp. 1380–1384.

Watt, N. F. "Five-Year Follow-Up of Geriatric Chronically Ill Mental Patients in Foster Home Care." *Journal of the American Geriatrics Society,* 18 (April 1970), pp. 310–316.

Wells, D. A., and Liebowitz, S. W. "Psychiatric Hospitalization for Senile Dementia." *Journal of the American Geriatrics Society,* 20 (August 1972), pp. 391–393.

Wetzel, J. W. "Interventions with the Depressed Elderly in Institutions." *Social Casework: The Journal of Contemporary Social Work,* 61 (April 1980), pp. 234–239.

Williams, J. R., Csalany, L., and Misevic, G. "Drug Therapy with or Without Group Discussion: Effects of Various Regimens on the Behavior of Geriatric Patients in a Mental Hospital." *Journal of the American Geriatrics Society,* 15 (January 1967), pp. 34–40.

Yood, B., and Davis, E. T. "Placement of Elderly Psychiatric Patients." *Geriatrics,* 24, No. 6 (1969), pp. 129–133.

Zarit, S. H.; Cole, K. D.; and Guider, R. L. "Memory Training Strategies and Subjective Complaints of Memory in the Aged." *The Gerontologist,* 21 (April 1981), pp. 158–164.

Zeller, F. A., and Knight, R. "Preventicare's Impact: Preliminary Results of a Survey." *Long Term Care and Health Services Administrative Quarterly,* 2, No. 1 (1978), pp. 5–19.

Health

Akabas, S. H.; Fine, M.; and Yasser, R. "Putting Secondary Prevention to the Test: A Study of an Early Intervention Strategy with Disabled Workers." *Journal of Primary Prevention,* 2, No. 3 (1982), pp. 165–187.

Beppler, M. C. "The Disabled Homemaker: Organizational Activities, Family Participation, and Rehabilitation Success." *Rehabilitation Literature,* 35, No. 7 (1974), pp. 200–206.

Berkman, B. "Psychosocial Problems and Outcome: An External Validity Study." *Health and Social Work,* 5 (August 1980), pp. 5–21.

Blatterbauer, S.; Kupst, M. J.; and Schulman, J. L. "Enhancing the Relationship Between Physician and Patient." *Health and Social Work,* 1 (February 1976), pp. 45–57.

Bozarth, J. D., and Rubin, S. E. "Empirical Observation of Rehabilitation Counselor Performance and Outcome: Some Implications." *Rehabilitation Counseling Bulletin,* 19 (September 1975), pp. 294–298.

Conyard, S.; Krishnamurthy, M.; and Dosik, H. "Psychosocial Aspects of Sickle-Cell Anemia in Adolescents." *Health and Social Work,* 5 (February 1980), pp. 20–26.

Coulton, C. J. *Social Work Quality Assurance Programs: A Comparative Analysis.* Washington, D.C.: National Association of Social Workers, 1979.

Dauber, B.; Zalar, M.; and Goldstein, P. J. "Abortion Counseling and Behavioral Change." *Family Planning Perspectives,* 4, No. 2 (1972), pp. 23–27.

Dillard, R. G.; Auerbach, K. G.; and Showalter, A. H. "A Parents' Program in the Intensive Care Nursery: Its Relationship to Maternal Attitudes and Expectations." *Social Work in Health Care,* 5 (Summer 1980), pp. 245–251.

Eisen, S. V., and Grob, M. C. "Assessing Consumer Satisfaction from Letters to the Hospital." *Hospital and Community Psychiatry,* 30 (May 1979), pp. 344–347.

Gentry, B. F., and Stevens, J. R. *Case Management in a Medical Assistance Program: Forsyth County.* Raleigh: North Carolina State Department of Social Services, 1972.

Gentry, M. E. *Early Detection and Treatment—Social Worker and Pediatricians in Private Practice.* Lexington: College of Social Professions, Kentucky University, 1977.

Hedblom, J. E.; Hubbard, F. A.; and Anderson, A. E. "Anorexia Nervosa:

A Multidisciplinary Treatment Program for Patient and Family." *Social Work in Health Care,* 7 (Winter 1981), pp. 67-86.

Hudgens, A. J. "Family-Oriented Treatment of Chronic Pain." *Journal of Marital and Family Therapy,* 5 (October 1979), pp. 67-78.

Institute for Public Health Social Workers. *Evaluation of Social Work Services in Community Health and Medical Care Programs: Based on the Proceedings of the 1973 Annual Institute for Public Health Social Workers.* Washington, D.C.: U.S. Department of Health, Education & Welfare, 1977.

Jackson, R. C., and Morton, J. *Evaluation of Social Work Services in Community Health and Medical Care Programs.* Berkeley: University of California, 1973.

Johnson, E. M., and Stark, D. E. "A Group Program for Cancer Patients and Their Family Members in an Acute Care Teaching Hospital." *Social Work in Health Care,* 5 (Fall 1980), pp. 335-349.

Kavaler, F., and Swire, M. R. "Health Services for Foster Children: An Evaluation of Agency Programs." *Child Welfare,* 53 (March 1974), pp. 147-157.

Kupst, M. J., et al. "Helping Parents Cope with the Diagnosis of Congenital Heart Defect: An Experimental Study." *Pediatrics,* 59 (1977), pp. 266-272.

Lang, P. A., and Oppenheimer, J. R. "The Influence of Social Work When Parents Are Faced with the Fatal Illness of a Child." *Social Casework,* 49 (March 1968), pp. 161-166.

Levenstein, P.; Kochman, A.; and Roth, H. A. "From Laboratory to Real World: Service Delivery of the Mother-Child Home Program." *American Journal of Orthopsychiatry,* 43 (January 1973), pp. 72-78.

Luborsky, L., et al. "Behavioral Versus Pharmacological Treatments for Essential Hypertension: A Pilot Study." *International Journal of Psychiatry in Medicine,* 10, No. 1 (1980-81), pp. 33-40.

Nagaraja, J. "Anorexia and Cyclic Vomiting in Children: A Psychogenic Study." *Child Psychiatry Quarterly,* 7, No. 4 (1974), pp. 1-5.

Ogren, E. H. "Sample Bias in Patient Evaluation of Hospital Social Services." *Social Work in Health Care,* 1 (Winter 1975), pp. 55-63.

Penick, S. B., et al. "Behavior Modification in the Treatment of Obesity." *Psychosomatic Medicine,* 33, No. 1 (1971), pp. 49-55.

Perlstadt, H., and Kozak, L. J. "Emergency Medicine." *Society,* 14, No. 2 (1977), pp. 41-46.

Phillip, C., and Siefert, K. "A Study of Maternal Participation in Preschool Programs for Handicapped Children and Their Families." *Social Work in Health Care,* 5 (Spring 1978), pp. 165–175.

Rahe, R. H.; O'Neil, T.; and Arthur, R. J. *Brief Group Therapy Following Myocardial Infarction. Eighteen-Month Follow-Up of a Controlled Trial.* San Diego, Calif.: Naval Health Resource Center, 1975.

Reed, J. W. "Rehabilitating the Chronically Ill: A 5-Year Follow-up of 341 Chronically Ill Ambulatory Medical Outpatients." *Journal of Chronic Diseases,* 20 (June 1967), pp. 457–468.

Resick, P. A., et al. "Social Adjustment in Victims of Sexual Assault." *Journal of Counseling and Clinical Psychology,* 49 (December 1981), pp. 705–712.

Rie, H. E., et al. "Immediate and Long-term Effects of Interventions Early in Prolonged Hospitalization." *Pediatrics,* 41, No. 4 (1968), pp. 755–764.

Rogow, S. M. "Developing Play Skills and Communicative Competence in Multiply Handicapped Young People." *Journal of Visual Impairment and Blindness,* 75 (May 1981), pp. 197–202.

Rosenberg, J. "Veterans' Perceptions of Their Hospital Care." *Social Work Research and Abstracts,* 13 (Fall 1977), pp. 30–34.

Schinke, S. P. "Evaluating Social Work Practice: A Conceptual Model and Example." *Social Casework: The Journal of Contemporary Social Work,* 60 (April 1979), pp. 195–200.

Sedge, S. K. "Assertiveness Training with Hearing-Impaired Persons." *Rehabilitation Counseling Bulletin,* 25 (March 1982), pp. 146–152.

Shewchuk, L. A., et al. "Preliminary Observations on an Intervention Program for Heavy Smokers." *International Journal of the Addictions,* 12, Nos. 2–3 (1977), pp. 323–336.

Skipper, J. K., Jr., and Leonard, R. C. "Children, Stress, and Hospitalization: A Field Experiment." *Journal of Health and Social Behavior,* 9 (December 1968), pp. 275–286.

Stevenson, K. M. "Obesity Treatment: Research Application." *Social Work in Health Care,* 4 (Spring 1978), pp. 165–178.

Stuart, R. B. "Behavioral Control of Overeating." *Behaviour Research and Therapy,* 5, No. 4 (1967), pp. 357–365.

Surwit, R. S.; Shapiro, D.; and Good, M. I. "Comparison of Cardiovascular Biofeedback, Neuromuscular Feedback, and Meditation in the Treatment of Borderline Essential Hypertension." *Journal of Consulting and Clinical Psychology,* 46 (April 1978), pp. 252–263.

Tasem, W. M.; Dasteel, J. C.; and Goldenberg, E. D. "Psychiatric Screening and Brief Intervention in a Pediatric Program Utilizing Allied Health Personnel." *American Journal of Orthopsychiatry*, 4 (July 1974), pp. 568–578.

Toseland, R. W.; Kabat, D.; and Kemp, K. "Evaluation of a Smoking-Cessation Group Treatment Program." *Social Work Research and Abstracts*, 19 (Spring 1983), pp. 12–19.

War Blinded Veterans in a Postwar Setting. A Social Work Followup of Rehabilitation Measures for Blinded Veterans with Service-Connected Disabilities Between December 7, 1941 and March 31, 1953. Unpublished report, 1958. Available through National Technical Information Service, Access No. PB 81-102758.

Welch, G. J. "The Treatment of Compulsive Vomiting and Obsessive Thoughts Through Graduated Response Delay, Response Prevention, and Cognitive Correction." *Journal of Behavior Therapy and Experimental Psychiatry*, 10, No. 1 (1979), pp. 77–82.

Wood, P. E., et al. "Group Counseling for Cancer Patients in a Community Hospital." *Psychosomatics*, 19 (September 1978), pp. 555–557.

Mental Health

Altman, H. "Collaborative Discharge Planning for the Deinstitutionalized." *Social Work*, 27 (September 1982), pp. 422–427.

Anderson, C. M., et al. "Impact of Therapist on Patient Satisfaction in Group Psychotherapy." *Comprehensive Psychiatry*, 13 (January 1972), pp. 33–40.

Anderson, J. D. "Growth Groups and Alienation: A Comparative Study of Rogerian Encounter, Self-Directed Encounter, and Gestalt." *Group and Organization Studies*, 3, No. 1 (1978), pp. 85–107.

Barbee, M. S.; Berry, K. L.; and Micek, L. A. "Relationship of Work Therapy to Psychiatric Length of Stay and Readmission." *Journal of Consulting and Clinical Psychology*, 33 (December 1969), pp. 735–738.

Barkley, A. L.; Pixley, F.; and Walker, C. "Industrial Therapy: A Study of Success Rates Over an Eight-Year Period." *Rehabilitation Literature*, 37 (October 1976), pp. 130–139 and 144.

Beard, J. H., Malamud, T. J., and Rossman, E. "Psychiatric Rehabilitation and Long-term Rehospitalization Rates: The Findings of Two Research Studies." *Schizophrenia Bulletin*, 4, No. 4 (1978), pp. 622–635.

Beatty, F. S., and Beatty, J. M. "An Evaluation of Psychotherapy at a

Community Mental Health Center." *Journal of Psychology,* 76 (1970), pp. 45-55.

Bednar, R. L., and Parker, C. A. "Client Susceptibility to Persuasion and Counseling Outcome." *Journal of Counseling Psychology,* 16 (October 1969), pp. 415-420.

Benney, C., et al. "Facilitating Functioning of Mentally Ill Young Adults." *Social Casework,* 52 (September 1971), pp. 420-431.

Berlin, S. "Cognitive-Behavioral Intervention for Problems of Self-Criticism Among Women." *Social Work Research and Abstracts,* 16 (Winter 1980), pp. 19-28.

―――. "Women and Self-Criticism." in S. Schinke, ed., *Behavioral Methods in Social Welfare: Helping Children, Adults and Families in Community Settings.* New York: Aldine Publishing Co., 1981.

Bookhammer, R. S., et al. "A Five-Year Clinical Follow-up Study of Schizophrenics Treated by Rosen's 'Direct Analysis' Compared with Controls." *American Journal of Psychiatry,* 123 (1966).

Boyd, J. L.; McGill, C. W.; and Fallon, I. R. "Family Participation in the Community Rehabilitation of Schizophrenics." *Hospital and Community Psychiatry,* 32 (September 1981), pp. 629-632.

Brooks, V. R. "Sex and Sexual Orientation as Variables in Therapists' Biases and Therapy Outcomes." *Clinical Social Work Journal,* 9 (Fall 1981), pp. 198-210.

Burnell, G. M., and Taylor, P. H. "Psychoeducational Programs for Problems in Living." *Health and Social Work,* 7 (Winter 1982), pp. 7-13.

Byers, E. S.; Cohen, S.; and Harshbarger, D. D. "Impact of Aftercare Services on Recidivism of Mental Hospital Patients." *Community Mental Health Journal,* 14 (Spring 1978), pp. 26-34.

Carkhuff, R. R., and Pierce, R. "Differential Effects of Therapist, Race, and Social Class upon Patient Depth of Self-Exploration in the Initial Clinical Interview." *Journal of Consulting Psychology,* 31, No. 6 (1967), pp. 632-634.

Carkhuff, R. R., and Truax, C. B. "Lay Mental Health Counseling: The Effects of Lay Group Counseling." *Journal of Consulting Psychology,* 29, No. 5 (1965), pp. 426-431.

Chwast, J., and Lurie, A. "The Resocialization of the Discharged Depressed Patient." *Canadian Psychiatric Association Journal,* 11 (special supplement) (1966), pp. 131-140.

Corney, R. H. "Social Work Effectiveness in the Management of Depressed

Women: A Clinical Trial." *Psychological Medicine,* 11, No. 2 (1981), pp. 417–423.

Criswell, J. H. "Community Roles in Psychiatric Rehabilitation." *Welfare in Review,* 8 (January–February 1970), pp. 8–15.

Cross, D. G., et al. "Short- and Long-term Follow-up of Clients Receiving Insight-Oriented Therapy and Behavior Therapy." *Journal of Consulting and Clinical Psychology,* 50 (February 1982), pp. 103–112.

Cross, D. G.; Sheehan, P. W.; and Khan, J. A. "Alternative Advice and Counsel in Psychotherapy." *Journal of Consulting and Clinical Psychology,* 48 (October 1980), pp. 615–625.

Dailey, W. J., and Ives, K. B. "Exploring Client Reactions to Agency Service." *Social Casework,* 59 (April 1978), pp. 233–245.

Davis, A. E.; Dinitz, S.; and Pasamanick, B. "The Prevention of Hospitalization in Schizophrenia: Five Years After an Experimental Program." *American Journal of Orthopsychiatry,* 42 (April 1972), pp. 375–388.

Donovan, J. M.; Bennett, M. J.; and McElroy, C. M. "The Crisis Group: An Outcome Study." *American Journal of Psychiatry,* 136 (July 1979), pp. 906–910.

Duehn, W. D., and Proctor, E. K. "Initial Clinical Interaction and Premature Discontinuance in Treatment." *American Journal of Orthopsychiatry,* 47 (April 1977), pp. 284–290.

Edwards, D. W., et al. "Developing Comparison Groups for Community Mental Health: The Utility of Community Surveys." *American Journal of Community Psychology,* 7 (February 1979), pp. 123–127.

Eisenthal, S., and Lazare, A. "Evaluation of the Initial Interview in a Walk-in Clinic: The Patient's Perspective on a 'Customer Approach.'" *Journal of Nervous and Mental Disease,* 162 (March 1976), pp. 169–176.

Ewalt, P. L., and Kutz, J. "An Examination of Advice-Giving as a Therapeutic Intervention." *Smith College Studies in Social Work,* 47 (November 1976), pp. 3–19.

Fago, D. P. "Time-Unlimited, Brief, and Longer-Term Psychotherapy with Rural Clients." *Journal of Rural Community Psychology,* 1, No. 2 (1980), pp. 16–23.

Fairweather, G. W., et al. *Community Life for the Mentally Ill.* Chicago: Aldine Publishing Co., 1969.

Fisher, T.; Nackman, N. S.; and Vyas, A. "Aftercare Services in a Family Agency." *Social Casework,* 54 (March 1973), pp. 131–140.

Fortune, A. E. "Communication in Task-Centered Treatment." *Social Work,* 24 (September 1979), pp. 390–396.

———. "Problem-Solving Processes in Task-Centered Treatment with Adults and Children." *Journal of Social Service Research,* 2 (Summer 1979), pp. 357–371.

Galassi, J. P.; Galassi, M. D.; and Litz, C. M. "Assertive Training in Groups Using Video Feedback." *Journal of Counseling Psychology,* 21 (October 1974), pp. 390–394.

Galassi, J. P.; Kostka, M. P.; and Galassi, M. D. "Assertive Training: A One Year Follow-Up." *Journal of Counseling Psychology,* 22 (October 1975), pp. 451–452.

Gibbons, J. S., et al. "Evaluation of a Social Work Service for Self-Poisoning Patients." *British Journal of Psychiatry,* 133 (1978), pp. 111–118.

Goldberg, S. C., et al. "Prediction of Relapse in Schizophrenic Outpatients Treated by Drug and Sociotherapy." *Archives of General Psychiatry,* 34 (February 1977), pp. 171–184.

Goldstein, E. G. "The Influence of Parental Attitudes on Psychiatric Treatment Outcome." *Social Casework: The Journal of Contemporary Social Work,* 60 (June 1979), pp. 350–359.

Goldstein, M. J., et al. "Drug and Family Therapy in the Aftercare of Acute Schizophrenics." *Archives of General Psychiatry,* 35 (October 1978), pp. 1169–1177.

Goldstein, M. J., et al. "Long-acting Phenothiazine and Social Therapy in the Community Treatment of Acute Schizophrenia." In M. Greenblatt, ed., *Drug in Combination with Other Therapies.* New York: Grune & Stratton, 1975, pp. 35–47.

Grad, J., and Sainsbury, P. "The Effects That Patients Have on Their Families in a Community-Care and a Control Psychiatric Service: A Two-Year Follow-Up." *British Journal of Psychiatry,* 114 (1968), pp. 265–278.

Grob, M. C.; Eisen, S. V.; and Edinburg, G. M. "Clinical Social Work with Young Adult Inpatients: Perspectives of Patients, Parents, and Clinicians." *Social Work in Health Care,* 8 (Spring 1982), pp. 1–9.

Gumrukcu, P. "The Efficacy of a Psychiatric Halfway House: A Three-Year Study of Therapeutic Residence." *Sociological Quarterly,* 9, No. 3 (1968), pp. 374–386.

Guy, W., et al. "A Controlled Evaluation of Day Hospital Effectiveness." *Archives of General Psychiatry,* 20 (March 1969), pp. 329–338.

Harty, M., and Horwitz, L. "Therapeutic Outcome as Rated by Patients,

Therapists, and Judges." *Archives of General Psychiatry,* 33 (August 1976), pp. 957–961.

Hayden, B. "Verbal and Therapeutic Styles and Experienced Therapists Who Differ in Peer-Rated Therapist Effectiveness." *Journal of Counseling Psychology,* 22 (October 1975), pp. 384–389.

Heap, R. F., et al. "Behavior-Milieu Therapy with Chronic Neuropsychiatric Patients." *Journal of Abnormal Psychology,* 76 (August 1970), pp. 349–354.

Hogarty, G. E., et al. "Drug and Sociotherapy in the Aftercare of Schizophrenic Patients: One-Year Relapse Rates." *Archives of General Psychiatry,* 28 (January 1973), pp. 54–69.

———. "Drug and Sociotherapy in the Aftercare of Schizophrenic Patients: II. Two-Year Relapse Rates." *Archives of General Psychiatry,* 31 (May 1974), pp. 603–608.

———. "Fluphenazine and Social Therapy in the Aftercare of Schizophrenic Patients." *Archives of General Psychiatry,* 36 (November 1979), pp. 1283–1294.

Hurst, J. C., et al. "Counselor-Client Diagnostic Agreement and Perceived Outcomes of Counseling." *Journal of Counseling Psychology,* 16 (October 1969), pp. 421–426.

Kahn, M. W., and Heiman, E. "Factors Associated with Number of Treatment Interviews of Patients from a Barrio Neighborhood Mental Health Service: A Cross-Validation." *American Journal of Community Psychology,* 7 (April 1979), pp. 231–235.

Kalafat, J.; Boroto, D. R.; and France, K. "Relationships Among Experience Level and Value Orientation and the Performance of Paraprofessional Telephone Counselors." *American Journal of Community Psychology,* 7 (April 1979), pp. 167–180.

Karp, H. N., and Karls, J. M. "Combining Crisis Therapy and Mental Health Consultation." *Archives of General Psychiatry,* 14 (May 1966), pp. 536–542.

Kaseman, B. M. "An Experimental Use of Structured Techniques in Group Psychotherapy." *Group Psychotherapy, Psychodrama and Sociometry,* 29 (1976), pp. 33–39.

Kelly, J. A., et al. "Objective Evaluation and Prediction of Client Improvement in Mental Health Aftercare." *Social Work in Health Care,* 5 (Spring 1979), pp. 187–202.

King, C. E., and Goldstein, M. J. "Therapist Ratings of Achievement of Objectives in Psychotherapy with Acute Schizophrenics." *Schizophrenia Bulletin,* 5, No. 1 (1979), pp. 118–129.

Kirk, S. A. "Effectiveness of Community Services for Discharged Mental Hospital Patients." *American Journal of Orthopsychiatry,* 46 (October 1976), pp. 646–659.

Kjenaas, M. A. "A Program to Improve Aftercare in a Rural Area." *Hospital and Community Psychiatry,* 31 (June 1980), pp. 401–403.

Koonce, G. M. "Social Work with Mental Patients in the Community." *Social Work,* 18 (May 1973), pp. 30–34.

LaFerriere, L., and Calsyn, R. "Goal Attainment Scaling: An Effective Treatment Technique in Short-Term Therapy." *American Journal of Community Psychology,* 6 (June 1978), pp. 271–282.

Lamb, H. R., and Goertzel, V. "High Expectations of Long-Term Ex-State Hospital Patients." *American Journal of Psychiatry,* 129 (April 1972), pp. 471–475.

Langsley, D. G.; Flomenhaft, K.; and Machotka, P. "Follow-up Evaluation of Family Crisis Therapy." *American Journal of Orthopsychiatry,* 39 (October 1969), pp. 753–758.

LaRoche, B.; Sigal, J. J.; and Grayson, M. "Collaboration Between a Police Force and the Psychiatric Service of a General Hospital: A Study of Outcome." *Canadian Journal of Criminology and Corrections,* 16 (April 1974), pp. 162–172.

Lawrence, H., and Walter, C. L. "Testing a Behavioral Approach with Groups." *Social Work,* 23 (April 1978), pp. 127–133.

Leader, M. A. "The Hillside Aftercare Apartment Project: A Pilot Follow-Up Study." *Social Work in Health Care,* 3 (Fall 1978), pp. 419–429.

Lewis, J., and Mider, P. A. "Effects of Leadership Style on Content and Work Styles of Short-Term Therapy Groups." *Journal of Counseling Psychology,* 20 (April 1973), pp. 137–141.

Linn, M. W., et al., "Day Treatment and Psychotropic Drugs in the Aftercare of Schizophrenic Patients." *Archives of General Psychiatry,* 36 (October 1979), pp. 1055–1066.

Linn, M. W., et al. "Hospital Versus Community (Foster) Care for Psychiatric Patients." *Archives of General Psychiatry,* 34 (January 1977), pp. 78–83.

Linn, M. W., Klett, C. J., and Caffey, E. M. "Foster Home Characteristics and Psychiatric Patient Outcome." *Archives of General Psychiatry,* 37 (1980), pp. 129–132.

Loeb, A., and Scoles, P. "Reactivating Dropouts from a Psychiatric Rehabilitation Program." *Social Work,* 13 (July 1968), pp. 48–54.

Maluccio, A. N. "Perspectives of Social Workers and Clients on Treatment Outcome." *Social Casework,* 60 (September 1979), pp. 394-401.

Mannino, F. V., and Shore, M. F. "Demonstrating Effectiveness in an Aftercare Program." *Social Work,* 19 (May 1974), pp. 351-354.

———. "Family Structure, Aftercare, and Post-Hospital Adjustment." *American Journal of Orthopsychiatry,* 44 (January 1974), pp. 76-85.

Marion, W. L., and Grabski, D. A. "An Assessment of a Continuing Care Program." *Hospital and Community Psychiatry,* 30 (June 1979), pp. 393-395.

Marks, J.; Sondona, B.; and Schalock, R. "Reinforcement Versus Relationship Therapy for Schizophrenics." *Journal of Abnormal Psychology,* 73 (November 1968), pp. 397-402.

Marx, A. J.; Test, M. A.; and Stein, L. I. "Extro-Hospital Management of Severe Mental Illness." *Archives of General Psychiatry,* 29 (April 1973), pp. 505-511.

Marziali, E.; Marmar, C.; and Krupnick, J. "Therapeutic Alliance Scales: Development and Relationship to Psychotherapy Outcome." *American Journal of Psychiatry,* 138 (March 1981), pp. 361-364.

Masnik, R.; Olarte, S. W.; and Rosen, A. "Coffee Groups: A Nine-Year Follow-Up Study." *American Journal of Psychiatry,* 137 (January 1980), pp. 91-93.

Mayer, J. E., and Rosenblatt, A. "Clash in Perspective Between Mental Patients and Staff." *American Journal of Orthopsychiatry,* 44 (April 1974), pp. 432-441.

McDonnell, D. "An Evaluation of Day Centre Care." *International Journal of Social Psychiatry,* 23, No. 2 (1977), pp. 110-119.

McLachlan, J. F. C. "Benefit from Group Therapy as a Function of Patient-Therapist Match on Conceptual Level." *Psychotherapy: Theory, Research and Practice,* 9, No. 4 (1972), pp. 317-323.

Mendelsohn, G. A., and Rankin, N. O. "Client-Counselor Compatibility and the Outcome of Counseling." *Journal of Abnormal Psychology,* 74 (May 1969), pp. 157-163.

Meyer, R. E.; Schiff, L. F.; and Becker, A. "The Home Treatment of Psychotic Patients: An Analysis of 154 Cases." *American Journal of Psychiatry,* 123 (January 1967), pp. 1430-1438.

Mintz, J.; O'Brien, C. P.; and Luborsky, L. "Predicting the Outcome of Psychotherapy for Schizophrenics: Relative Contributions of Patient, Therapist, and Treatment Characteristics." *Archives of General Psychiatry,* 33 (October 1976), pp. 1183-1186.

Mosher, L. R. "A Research Design for Evaluating a Psychosocial Treatment of Schizophrenia." *Hospital and Community Psychiatry,* 23 (August 1972), pp. 229-234.

Mosher, L. R., and Menn, A. Z. "Community Resident Treatment for Schizophrenia: Two-Year Follow-Up." *Hospital and Community Psychiatry,* 29 (November 1978), pp. 715-723.

———. "Lowered Barriers in the Community: The Soteria Model." In L. I. Stein and M. A. Test, eds., *Alternatives to Mental Hospital Treatment.* New York: Plenum Press, 1978, pp. 57-74.

Mosher, L. R., Menn, A., and Matthews, S. M. "Soteria: Evaluation of a Home-Based Treatment for Schizophrenia." *American Journal of Orthopsychiatry,* 45 (April 1975), pp. 455-467.

Mosher, L. R.; Rufman, A.; and Menn, A. "Characteristics of Nonprofessionals Serving as Primary Therapists for Acute Schizophrenia." *Hospital and Community Psychiatry,* 24 (June 1973), pp. 391-395.

Muench, G. A. "An Investigation of the Efficacy of Time-limited Psychotherapy." *Journal of Counseling Psychology,* 12 (July 1965), pp. 294-299.

Nuehring, E. M., and Ladner, R. A. "Use of Aftercare Programs in Community Mental Health Clinics." *Social Work Research and Abstracts,* 16 (Spring 1980), pp. 34-40.

O'Brien, C. P., et al., "Groups Versus Individual Psychotherapy with Schizophrenics." *Archives of General Psychiatry,* 27 (April 1972), pp. 474-478.

Orlinsky, D. E., and Howard, K. I. "The Good Therapy Hour: Experiential Correlates of Patients' and Therapists' Evaluations of Therapy Sessions." *Archives of General Psychiatry,* 16 (May 1967), pp. 621-632.

Parad, H. J., and Parad, L. G. "A Study of Crisis-oriented Planned Short-term Treatment: Parts I and II." *Social Casework,* 49 (June 1968), pp. 346-355, and (September 1968), pp. 418-426.

Peterson, C. L. "A Comparative Study of Referral Success in First Appointments Made by Patients and by Staff." *Hospital and Community Psychiatry,* 32 (November 1981), pp. 800-801.

Pierce, R. M., and Drasgow, J. "Teaching Facilitative Interpersonal Functioning to Psychiatric Inpatients." *Journal of Counseling Psychology,* 16 (July 1969), pp. 295-298.

Piper, W. E.; Debbane, E. G., and Garant, J. "An Outcome Study of Group Therapy." *Archives of General Psychiatry,* 34 (September 1977), pp. 1027-1032.

———. "Group Psychotherapy Outcome Research: Problems and Prospects of a First-Year Project." *International Journal of Group Psychotherapy,* 27, No. 3 (1977), pp. 321-341.

Polak, P. R. "A Comprehensive System of Alternatives to Psychiatric Hospitalization." In L. I. Stein and M. A. Test, eds., *Alternatives to Mental Hospital Treatment.* New York: Plenum Press, 1978, pp. 115-137.

Polak, P. R., et al. "Prevention in Mental Health: A Controlled Study." *American Journal of Psychiatry,* 132 (February 1975), pp. 146-149.

Polak, P. R., and Kirby, M. "A Model to Replace Psychiatric Hospitals." *Journal of Nervous and Mental Disease,* 162, No. 1 (1976), pp. 13-22.

Poser, E. G. "The Effect of Therapists' Training on Group Therapeutic Outcome." *Journal of Consulting Psychology,* 30 (August 1966), pp. 283-289.

Purvis, S. A., and Miskimins, R. W. "Effects of Community Follow-up on Post-hospital Adjustment of Psychiatric Patients." *Community Mental Health Journal,* 6, No. 5 (1970), pp. 374-382.

Reid, W. J. "A Test of a Task-Centered Approach." *Social Work,* 20 (January 1975), pp. 3-9.

———. *The Task-Centered System.* New York: Columbia University Press, 1978.

Reid, W. J., and Epstein, L. *Task-Centered Casework.* New York: Columbia University Press, 1972.

Reid, W. J., and Shyne, A. W. *Brief and Extended Casework.* New York: Columbia University Press, 1969.

Richey, C. A. "Assertiveness Training for Women." In S. P. Schinke, ed., *Behavioral Methods in Social Welfare: Helping Children, Adults and Families in Community Settings.* New York: Aldine Publishing Co., 1981.

Riehman, L., and O'Brien, C. F. "Project in Apartment Group Living." *Social Work,* 18 (May 1973), pp. 36-43.

Rose, S. D. "How Group Attributes Relate to Outcome in Behavior Group Therapy." *Social Work Research and Abstracts,* 17 (Fall 1981), pp. 25-29.

———. "In Pursuit of Social Competence." *Social Work,* 20 (January 1975), pp. 33-39.

———. "The Effect of Contingency Contracting on the Completion Rate of Behavior Assignments in Assertion Training Groups." *Journal of Social Service Research,* 1 (Spring 1978), pp. 299-305.

Rosen, A., and Lieberman, D. "The Experimental Evaluation of Interview Performance of Social Workers." *Social Service Review,* 46 (September 1972), pp. 395-412.

Rosen, B., et al. "Clinical Effectiveness of 'Short' Versus 'Long' Psychiatric Hospitalization: I. Inpatient Results." *Archives of General Psychiatry,* 33 (November 1976), pp. 1316-1322.

Rosenberg, G., and Cotloff, P. "A Community Participation Program for the Hospitalized Mental Patient." *Journal of Jewish Communal Service,* 43 (Spring 1967), pp. 253-259.

Roskin, M. "Coping with Life Changes—A Preventive Social Work Approach." *American Journal of Community Psychology,* 10 (June 1982), pp. 331-339.

Ro-Trock, K. G., Wellisch, D. K., and Schoolar, J. C. "A Family Therapy Outcome Study in an Inpatient Setting." *American Journal of Orthopsychiatry,* 47 (July 1977), pp. 514-522.

Sainsbury, E.; Nixon, S.; and Phillips, D. *Social Work in Focus: Clients' and Social Workers' Perceptions in Long-term Social Work.* London, England: Routledge & Kegan Paul, 1982.

Schainblatt, A. H. "What Happens to the Clients?" *Community Mental Health Journal,* 16 (Winter 1980), pp. 331-342.

Schinke, S. P., and Rose, S. D. "Interpersonal Skill Training in Groups." *Journal of Counseling Psychology,* 23 (October 1976), pp. 442-448.

Shattan, S. P., et al. "Group Treatment of Conditionally Discharged Patients in a Mental Health Clinic." *American Journal of Psychiatry,* 122 (July 1966), pp. 798-805.

Shenoy, R. S.; Shires, B. W.; and White, M. S. "Using a Schiz-Anon Group in the Treatment of Chronic Ambulatory Schizophrenics." *Hospital and Community Psychiatry,* 32 (June 1981), pp. 421-422.

Shulman, L. "A Study of Practice Skills." *Social Work,* 23 (July 1978), pp. 274-280.

Sifneos, P. E. "Ongoing Outcome Research on Short-Term Dynamic Psychotherapy." *Psychotherapy and Psychosomatics,* 33, No. 4 (1980), pp. 233-241.

Simons, L. S., et al. "Treatment Outcome and Follow-Up Evaluation Based on Client Case Records in a Mental Health Center." *Journal of Consulting and Clinical Psychology,* 46 (April 1978), pp. 246-251.

Singh, R. N. "Brief Interviews: Approaches, Techniques, and Effectiveness." *Social Casework: The Journal of Contemporary Social Work,* 63 (December 1982), pp. 599-606.

Sirles, E. A. "Client-Counselor Agreement on Problem and Change." *Social Casework: The Journal of Contemporary Social Work,* 63 (June 1982), pp. 348-353.

Smith, W. G. "Evaluation of the Clinical Services of a Regional Mental Health Center." *Community Mental Health Journal,* 11 (Spring 1975), pp. 47-57.

Stein, L. I., and Test, M. A. "An Alternative to Mental Hospital Treatment." In Stein and Test, eds., *Alternatives to Mental Hospital Treatment.* New York: Plenum Press, 1978, pp. 43-55.

———. "An Alternative to Mental Hospital Treatment, I. Conceptual Model, Treatment Program, and Clinical Evaluation." *Archives of General Psychiatry,* 37 (April 1980), pp. 392-397.

———. "An Alternative to Mental Hospital Treatment, III. Social Cost." *Archives of General Psychiatry,* 37 (April 1980), pp. 409-412.

———. "A Community Treatment Program." *Hospital and Community Psychiatry,* 25 (October 1974), pp. 669-672.

———. "Retraining Hospital Staff for Work in a Community Program in Wisconsin." *Hospital and Community Psychiatry,* 27 (April 1976), pp. 266-268.

———. "Training in Community Living: Research Design and Results." In Stein and Test, eds., *Alternatives to Mental Hospital Treatment.* New York: Plenum Press, 1978, pp. 57-74.

Swenson, W. M., and Martin, H. R. "A Description and Evaluation of an Outpatient Intensive Psychotherapy Center." *American Journal of Psychiatry,* 133 (September 1976), pp. 1043-1046.

Tessler, R. C., and Polansky, N. "Perceived Similarity: A Paradox in Interviewing." *Social Work,* 20 (September 1975), pp. 359-363.

Toseland, R.; Krebs, A.; and Vahsen, J. "Changing Group Interaction Patterns." *Journal of Social Service Research,* 2 (Winter 1978), pp. 219-232.

Treger, H.; Thomson, D.; and Jaeack, G. S. "A Police-Social Work Team Model: Some Preliminary Findings and Implications for System Change." *Crime and Delinquency,* 20, No. 3 (1974), pp. 281-290.

Velasquez, J. S., and McCubbin, H. I. "Towards Establishing the Effectiveness of Community-Based Residential Treatment: Program Evaluation by Experimental Research." *Journal of Social Service Research,* 3 (Summer 1980), pp. 337-359.

Watson, G. G.; Fulton, J. R.; and Gurel, L. "Project Anchor: A Study of an Unsuccessful Volunteer Program to Help Former Patients."

Hospital and Community Psychiatry, 26 (March 1975), pp. 146-151.

Weinman, B., and Kleiner, R. J. "The Impact of Community Living and Community Member Intervention on the Adjustment of the Chronic Psychotic Patient." In L. I. Stein and M. A. Test, eds., *Alternatives to Mental Hospital Treatment.* New York: Plenum Press, 1978, pp. 139-159.

Weissman, M. M., et al. "Treatment Effects on the Social Adjustment of Depressed Patients." *Archives of General Psychiatry,* 30 (June 1974), pp. 771-778.

Weissman, M. M.; Geanakoplos, E.; and Prusoff, B. "Social Class and Attrition in Depressed Outpatients." *Social Casework,* 54 (March 1973), pp. 162-170.

Williams, J. S.; Dudley, H. K., Jr.; and Guinn, T. J. "Use of Day Treatment Center Concepts with State Hospital Inpatients." *American Journal of Orthopsychiatry,* 39 (October 1969), pp. 748-752.

Williams, R. I., and Blanton, R. L. "Verbal Conditioning in a Psychotherapeutic Situation." *Behaviour Research and Therapy,* 6, No. 1 (1968), pp. 97-103.

Wolford, J. A., et al. "The Effect on State Hospitalization of a Community Mental Health/Mental Retardation Center." *American Journal of Psychiatry,* 129 (February 1972), pp. 202-206.

Wolkon, G. H.; Karmen, M.; and Tanaka, H. T. "Evaluation of a Social Rehabilitation Program for Recently Released Psychiatric Patients." *Community Mental Health Journal,* 7 (Winter 1971), pp. 312-322.

Wolkon, G. H., and Tanaka, H. T. "Outcome of a Social Rehabilitation Service for Released Psychiatric Patients: A Descriptive Study." *Social Work,* 11 (April 1966), pp. 53-61.

Organizational Effectiveness

Aram, J. D., and Stratton, W. E. "The Development of Interagency Cooperation." *Social Service Review,* 48 (September 1974), pp. 412-421.

Baker, S., and Vosburgh, W. W. "Workers, Cases, and Errors: The Effect of Work Load on Errors in Public Assistance Eligibility Determinations." *Administration in Social Work,* 1 (Summer 1977), pp. 161-170.

Buffman, W. E., and Konick, A. "Employees' Job Satisfaction, Residents' Functioning, and Treatment Progress in Psychiatric Institutions." *Health and Social Work,* 7 (Fall 1982), pp. 320-327.

Carzo, R., Jr., and Yanouzas, J. N. "Effects of Flat and Tall Organization

Structure." *Administrative Science Quarterly,* 14 (June 1969), pp. 178-191.

Cubero, A. V., and Porto, H. R. *Improved Services to Puerto Ricans: End of Project Report.* Vol. 1. New York: Puerto Rican Inter-Agency Council, 1975.

Ellsworth, R., et al. "Milieu Characteristics of Successful Psychiatric Treatment Programs." *American Journal of Orthopsychiatry,* 41 (April 1971), pp. 427-441.

Greenley, J. R., and Schoenherr, R. A. "Organization Effects on Client Satisfaction with Humaneness of Service." *Journal of Health and Social Behavior,* 22 (March 1981), pp. 2-18.

Grinnell, R. M., Jr., and Hill, L. S. "Do Agency Administrative Changes Affect the Effectiveness and Efficiency of DHR Employees?" *Journal of Sociology and Social Welfare,* 6 (June 1979), pp. 503-508.

Hasenfeld, Y. "Organizational Dilemmas in Innovating Social Services: The Case of the Community Action Centers." *Journal of Health and Social Behavior,* 12 (Fall 1971), pp. 208-216.

Holland, T. P., et al. "Institutional Structure and Resident Outcomes." *Journal of Health and Social Behavior,* 22 (December 1981), pp. 433-444.

Marcos, L. R., and Gil, R. M. "Muddling Through Mental Health Policies." *American Journal of Psychiatry,* 140 (July 1983), pp. 853-856.

Morgenbesser, M., et al. "The Evolution of Three Alternative Social Service Agencies." *Catalyst,* 3, No. 3 (1981), pp. 71-83.

Norman, E. C., and Forti, T. J. "A Study of the Process and the Outcome of Mental Health Consultation." *Community Mental Health Journal,* 8 (Winter 1972), pp. 261-270.

Schwartz, E. E., and Sample, W. C. "First Findings from Midway." *Social Service Review,* 41 (June 1967), pp. 113-151.

Weinman, M. L., et al. "Organizational Structure and Effectiveness in General Hospital Psychiatry Departments." *Administration in Mental Health,* 7 (Fall 1979), pp. 32-41.

Wolins, M., Wozner, Y., and Shye, S. "Rejuvenating the Asylum: A Field Study." *Social Work Research and Abstracts,* 16 (Spring 1980), pp. 17-25.

Zalba, S. R., and Stein, H. D. *Assessing Organizational Effectiveness: The Development of a Methodology for Assessing the Organizational Effectiveness of the Social Service Agency.* Cleveland, Ohio: Case Western Reserve University, School of Applied Social Sciences, 1969.

Public Social Services

Andrews, M. P., and Swanson, J. F. *An Evaluation of Parent Aide Programs.* Lansing: Michigan State Department of Social Services, 1979.

Behling, J. *An Experimental Study to Measure the Effectiveness of Casework Service.* Columbus, Ohio: Franklin County Welfare Department, 1961.

Benn, B. A., and Wickberg, B. *Project on Relative Effectiveness of Social Services in Minnesota: Findings of the Third Year.* St. Paul: Minnesota Department of Public Welfare, 1973.

Brown, G. E., ed. *The Multi-Problem Dilemma: A Social Research Demonstration with Multi-Problem Families.* Metuchen, N.J.: Scarecrow Press, 1968.

Buchanan, S. W., and Makofsky, L. R. "The Fearlessness of Revision. Attitudes of Clients Toward a Public Welfare Agency and a Community's Service." *Public Welfare,* 28 (Spring 1970), pp. 141-149.

Burlington-Morrisville Public Social Services Project: Evaluation. Final Report. Waterbury, N.Y.: Vermont Agency of Human Services, Planning Division, 1974.

Carlile, C., and Clement, D. J. *Lummi Indian Demonstration Project.* Olympia: Washington Department of Social and Health Services, 1973.

Dickerson, L. R.; Greenwood, R.; and Muthard, J. E. "A New Way Out for Welfare Recipients." *Social and Rehabilitation Record,* 2, No. 3 (1975), pp. 24-30.

Eppley, D. "How Effective Are Social Services?" *Social and Rehabilitation Record,* 2, No. 7 (1975), pp. 10-14.

Epstein, N., and Shainline, A. "Paraprofessional Parent-Aides and Disadvantaged Families." *Social Casework,* 55 (April 1974), pp. 230-236.

Evaluation of Pilot Project in the Rehabilitation of Dependent Families. Wilmington: Community Services Council of Delaware, 1966.

Evaluation of the Oregon Project for the Differential Use of Staff. Salem: Oregon State Public Welfare Division, Social Services Department, 1969.

Fiene, R., and Douglas, E. *Making the Almost Impossible—Possible: Evaluation of Human Services.* Harrisburg: Pennsylvania State Department of Public Welfare, 1978.

Foley, F. A. "Family Day Care for Children." *Children,* 13 (July-August 1966), pp. 141-144.

Friedman, J., and Weinberg, D. H. "The Great Housing Experiment."

In Friedman and Weinberg, eds., *Urban Affairs Annual Review,* Vol. 24. Beverly Hills, Calif.: Sage Publications, 1983.

Geismar, L. L. "Implications of a Family Life Improvement Project." *Social Casework,* 52 (July 1971), pp. 455-465.

———. *The Forgotten Neighborhood.* Metuchen, N.J.: Scarecrow Press, 1967.

———. "Thirteen Evaluative Studies." In E. J. Mullen and J. R. Dumpson, eds., *Evaluation of Social Intervention.* San Francisco: Jossey-Bass, 1972.

Geismar, L. L., et al. *Early Supports for Family Life: A Social Work Experiment.* Metuchen, N.J.: Scarecrow Press, 1972.

Geismar, L. L., and Ayres, B. *Patterns of Change in Problem Families: A Study of the Social Functioning and Movement of 150 Families Served by the Family-Centered Project.* St. Paul, Minn.: Family-Centered Project, Greater St. Paul Community Chest and Council, 1980.

Geismar, L. L., and Krisberg, J. "The Family Life Improvement Project: An Experiment in Preventive Intervention: Part I." *Social Casework,* 47 (November 1966), pp. 563-570.

———. "The Family Life Improvement Project: An Experiment in Preventive Intervention: Part II." *Social Casework,* 47 (December 1966), pp. 663-667.

Gibelman, M. "Are Clients Served Better When Services Are Purchased?" *Public Welfare,* 39 (Fall 1981), pp. 26-33.

Gilbert, N., and Specht, H. "Quantitative Aspects of Social Service Coordination Effects: Is More Better?" *Administration in Social Work,* 1 (Spring 1977), pp. 53-61.

Glickman, E. "Professional Social Work with Headstart Mothers." *Children,* 15 (March-April 1968), pp. 59-64.

Henderson, G. "Raising the Level of Children's Aspirations." *Children,* 12 (September-October 1965), pp. 195-199.

Hewett, K., et al. *Design Report Draft Evaluation of the Child and Family Resource Program, Volume I.* Washington, D.C.: Administration for Children, Youth and Families, U.S. Department of Health, Education & Welfare, 1979.

Iberg, L. *Collection of Papers Prepared for the Chemung County Research Demonstration with Dependent Multi-Problem Families.* New York: New York State Communities Aid Association, 1966.

Integrated Service Delivery. Olympia: Washington Department of Social and Health Services, 1975.

Kuhl, P. H. *The Family Center Project and Action Research on Socially Deprived Families.* Copenhagen, Denmark: The Danish National Institute of Social Research, 1969.

Lawrence, H. "Comparative Group Leadership Styles with Welfare Mothers." *Public Welfare,* 30 (Summer 1972), pp. 39–47.

Marin, R. C. *Family-Centered Treatment Research and Demonstration Project in Puerto Rico with Dependent Multiproblem Families: Final Report 1965–1966.* Rio Piedras: University of Puerto Rico School of Social Work, 1967.

McBroom, E. "Helping AFDC Families: A Comparative Study." *Social Service Review,* 39 (December 1965), pp. 390–398.

McClure, D., and Stephenson, A. *A Comparative Evaluation of Entry Level Social Work Experience of Social Work Majors and Non-Social Work Majors Graduated from the University of Kentucky in Kentucky State Social Welfare Agencies.* Frankfort: Kentucky Department for Human Resources, 1970.

McDonald, T. P., and Piliavin, I. "Impact of Separation on Community Social Service Utilization." *Social Service Review,* 55 (December 1981), pp. 628–635.

Morris, B. "Crisis Intervention in a Public Welfare Agency." *Social Casework,* 49 (December 1968), pp. 612–617.

Mullen, E. J.; Chazin, R. M.; and Feldstein, D. M. *Preventing Chronic Dependency.* New York: Community Service Society, 1979.

———. "Services for the Newly Dependent: An Assessment." *Social Service Review,* 46 (September 1972), pp. 309–322.

Munro, J. N., and Bach, T. R. "Effect of Time-Limited Counseling on Client Change." *Journal of Counseling Psychology,* 22 (October 1975), pp. 395–398.

Nelson, B. J. "Clients and Bureaucracies: Applicant Evaluations of Public Human Service and Benefit Programs." Unpublished manuscript, prepared for delivery at the Annual Meeting of the American Political Science Association, Washington, D.C., 1979.

Nelson, H. Y.; Jacoby, G. P.; and Shannon, T. M. "Evaluation of Homemaking and Consumer Education Programs for Low-Income Adults." *Home Economics Research Journal,* 6, No. 3 (1978), pp. 223–241.

Olson, I. "Some Effects of Increased Aid in Money and Social Services to Families Getting AFDC Grants." *Child Welfare,* 49 (February 1970), pp. 94–100.

Piliavin, I., and Gross, A. E. "The Effects of Separation of Services and Income Maintenance on AFDC Recipients." *Social Service Review,* 51 (September 1977), pp. 389-406.

Program Administration Review: Evaluating State Agency Casework as Reflected in Cases Closed as Employed During July 1, 1961-June 30, 1962. Washington, D.C.: Vocational Rehabilitation Administration, U.S. Department of Health, Education & Welfare, 1964.

Randall, R. "Social Services in AFDC: Steps Toward Evaluation." *Social Service Review,* 49 (June 1975), pp. 191-207.

Seaberg, J., and Bell, M. "Evaluation of Broad-Scale Service Networks." *Social Work Research and Abstracts,* 14 (Spring 1978), pp. 19-24.

Smith, D. W. *Guidelines for the Delivery of Social Health and Rehabilitation Services at the Community Level: An Exploratory Evaluation.* Tucson: University of Arizona, 1968.

Tableman, B., et al. "Stress Management Training for Women and Public Assistance." *American Journal of Community Psychology,* 10 (July 1982), pp. 357-367.

Total Package of Integrated Social and Rehabilitation Services: Anacostia Project: Final Report. Washington, D.C.: Government of the District of Columbia, Department of Human Resources, 1974.

Wagner, M. *Denmark's National Family Guidance Program: A Preventive Mental Health Program for Children and Families.* Rockville, Md.: National Institute of Mental Health, 1978.

Wallace, D. "The Chemung County Evaluation of Casework Service to Dependent Multiproblem Families: Another Problem Outcome." *Social Service Review,* 41 (December 1967), pp. 379-389.

Weller, L., and Luchterhand, E. "Effects of Improved Housing on the Family Functioning of Large, Low-Income Black Families." *Social Problems,* 20 (February 1973), pp. 382-389.

Wilkinson, K. P., and Ross, P. J. "Evaluation of the Mississippi AFDC Experiment." *Social Service Review,* 46 (September 1972), pp. 363-377.

Wilson, R. *Evaluation of a Pilot Project in the Rehabilitation of Dependent Families.* Wilmington: Community Services Council of Delaware, 1966.

Zimmerman, S. L. "Public Policies and Family Outcomes: Empirical Evidence or Ideology?" *Social Casework: The Journal of Contemporary Social Work,* 64 (March 1983), pp. 138-146.

Substance Abuse

Anglin, M. D.; McGlothlin, W. H.; and Speckart, G. "The Effect of Parole on Methadone Patient Behavior." *American Journal of Drug and Alcohol Abuse,* 8, No. 2 (1981), pp. 153-170.

Bartlett, D. P., and Intagliata, J. "Integration of Quality Assurance and Program Evaluation Activities in Alcoholism Treatment Programs: Part I." *Quality Review Bulletin,* 5 (November 1979), pp. 24-28.

———. "Integration of Quality Assurance and Program Evaluation Activities in Alcoholism Treatment Programs: Part II." *Quality Review Bulletin,* 6 (January 1980), pp. 17-22.

Bolman, W. M. "Abstinence Versus Permissiveness in the Psychotherapy of Alcoholism." *Archives of General Psychiatry,* 12 (May 1965), pp. 456-463.

Boscarino, J. "A National Survey of Alcoholism Treatment Centers in the United States—A Preliminary Report." *American Journal of Drug and Alcohol Abuse,* 7, Nos. 3-4 (1980), pp. 403-411.

Bowen, W. T., and Androes, L. "A Follow-up Study of 79 Alcoholic Patients: 1963-1965." *Bulletin of the Menninger Clinic,* 31 (January 1968), pp. 26-34.

Brill, L. "Three Approaches to the Casework Treatment of Narcotics Addicts." *Social Work,* 13 (April 1968), pp. 25-35.

Bromet, E., et al. "Posttreatment Functioning of Alcoholic Patients: Its Relation to Program Participation." *Journal of Consulting and Clinical Psychology,* 45 (October 1977), pp. 829-842.

Burton, G., and Kaplan, H. M. "Group Counseling in Conflicted Marriages Where Alcoholism Is Present: Clients' Evaluation of Effectiveness." *Journal of Marriage and the Family,* 30 (February 1968), pp. 74-79.

———. "Marriage Counseling with Alcoholics and Their Spouses: II. The Correlation of Excessive Drinking Behavior with Family Pathology and Social Deterioration." *British Journal of Addiction,* 63, Nos. 3-4 (1968), pp. 161-170.

Burton, G.; Kaplan, H. M.; and Hudd, E. H. "Marriage Counseling with Alcoholics and Their Spouses: I. A Critique of the Methodology of a Follow-up Study." *British Journal of Addiction,* 63, Nos. 3-4 (1968), pp. 151-160.

Cahill, C. A. "A Community Program for Control of Alcoholism." *Community Mental Health Journal,* 3 (Fall 1967), pp. 273-275.

Cannon, D. S., and Baker, T. B. "Emetic and Electric Shock Alcohol Aversion Therapy: Assessment of Conditioning." *Journal of Consulting and Clinical Psychology,* 49 (February 1981), pp. 20-33.

Cohen, P. C., and Krause, M. S., eds. *Casework with Wives of Alcoholics.* New York: Family Service Association of America, 1971.

Cole, S. G., and Cole, E. A. "Alcohol and Drug Abuse Treatment: Perceived Effectiveness of Inpatient Combined Treatment Programs." *American Journal of Drug and Alcohol Abuse,* 6, No. 1 (1979), pp. 109–123.

Coombs, R. H. "Back on the Streets: Therapeutic Communities' Impact upon Drug Users." *American Journal of Alcohol and Drug Abuse,* 8, No. 2 (1981), pp. 185–201.

Copemann, C. D., and Shaw, P. L. "A Behaviorally Oriented Treatment Program for Drug Addiction: A Preliminary Report." *American Journal of Public Health,* 66 (March 1976), pp. 286–287.

Davidson, A. F. "An Evaluation of the Treatment and Aftercare of 100 Alcoholics." *British Journal of Addiction,* 71 (September 1976), pp. 217–224.

Del Campo, E. J.; St. John, D.; and Kauffman, C. C. "Evaluation of the 21-Day Outpatient Heroin Detoxification." *International Journal of the Addictions,* 12, No. 7 (1977), pp. 923–935.

Ditman, K. S., et al. "A Controlled Experiment on the Use of Court Probation for Drunk Arrests." *American Journal of Psychiatry,* 124 (February 1967), pp. 160–163.

Dubourg, G. O. "After-care for Alcoholics—A Follow-up Study." *British Journal of Addiction,* 64 (June 1969), pp. 155–163.

Duehn, W. D., and Shannon, C. "Covert Sensitization in the Public High School: Short-Term Group Treatment of Male Adolescent Drug Abusers." *School Social Work Journal,* 1 (Spring 1974), pp. 27–35.

Edwards, D. W. "Spouse Participation in the Treatment of Alcoholism: Completion of Treatment and Recidivism." *Social Work with Groups,* 5 (Spring 1982), pp. 4–48.

Eldred, C. A.; Grier, V. V.; and Berliner, N. "Comprehensive Treatment for Heroin-Addicted Mothers." *Social Casework,* 55 (October 1974), pp. 470–477.

Ewing, J. A., and Rouse, B. A. "Failure of an Experimental Treatment Program to Inculcate Controlled Drinking in Alcoholics." *British Journal of Addiction,* 71 (June 1976), pp. 123–134.

Finlay, D. "Changing Problem Drinkers." *Social Work Research and Abstracts,* 13 (Winter 1977), pp. 30–37.

Gallant, D. M., et al. "The Value of a 'First Contact' Group Intake Session in an Alcoholism Outpatient Clinic: Statistical Confirmation." *Psychosomatics,* 7 (December 1966), pp. 349–352.

Gallen, M. "Prediction of Improvement in Two Contrasting Alcoholism

Treatment Programs." *Newsletter for Research in Mental Health and Behavioral Sciences,* 18, No. 2 (1976), pp. 31-32.

———, et al. "A Short-Term Follow-Up of Two Contrasting Alcoholic Treatment Programs: A Preliminary Report." *Newsletter for Research in Mental Health and Behavioral Sciences,* 15, No. 4 (1973), pp. 36-37.

Green, M., et al. "Outcomes of Pregnancy for Addicts Receiving Comprehensive Care." *American Journal of Drug and Alcohol Abuse,* 6, No. 4 (1979), pp. 413-429.

Homonoff, E., and Stephen, A. "Alcohol Education for Children of Alcoholics in a Boston Neighborhood." *Journal of Studies on Alcohol,* 40 (September 1979), pp. 923-926.

Jaffe, J. H.; Zaks, M. S.; and Washington, E. N. "Experience with the Use of Methadone in a Multi-Modality Program for the Treatment of Narcotics Users." *International Journal of the Addictions,* 4, No. 3 (1969), pp. 481-490.

Jansen, C. "Families in the Treatment of Alcoholism." *Journal of Studies on Alcohol,* 38 (January 1977), pp. 114-130.

Katz, L. "Salvation Army's Social Service Center: I. Program." *Quarterly Journal of Studies on Alcohol,* 25, No. 3 (1964), pp. 324-332.

———. "Salvation Army Men's Social Service Center: II. Results." *Quarterly Journal of Studies on Alcohol,* 27, No. 5 (1966), pp. 636-647.

King, B. L.; Bissell, L.; and O'Brien, P. "Alcoholics Anonymous, Alcoholism Counseling, and Social Work Treatment." *Health and Social Work,* 4 (Fall 1979), pp. 181-198.

Kish, G. B.; Ellsworth, R. B.; and Woody, M. M. "Effectiveness of an 84-Day and a 60-Day Alcoholism Treatment Program." *Journal of Studies on Alcohol,* 41 (January 1980), pp. 81-85.

Krause, M. S.; Breedlove, J. L.; and Bonnifare, K. F. "An Evaluation of the Results of Treatment." In P. C. Cohen and M. S. Krause, eds., *Casework with Wives of Alcoholics.* New York: Family Service Association of America, 1971.

Kurland, A. A., et al. "Psychedelic Therapy Utilizing LSD in the Treatment of the Alcoholic Patient: A Preliminary Report." *American Journal of Psychiatry,* 123 (October 1967), pp. 1210-1219.

Lanyon, R. I.; Primo, R. V.; and Wener, A. "An Aversion-Desensitization Treatment for Alcoholism." *Journal of Consulting and Clinical Psychology,* 38 (June 1972), pp. 394-398.

Lowe, W. C., and Thomas, S. D. "Assessing Alcoholism Treatment Effectiveness: A Comparison of Three Evaluative Measures." *Journal of Studies on Alcohol,* 37 (July 1976), pp. 883-889.

Mayer, J., et al. "Treatment of the Female Alcoholic: The Former Prisoner." *American Journal of Orthopsychiatry,* 37 (October 1967), pp. 932-937.

Meeks, D. E., and Kelly, C. "Family Therapy with the Families of Recovering Alcoholics." *The Social Worker-Le Travailleur Social,* 39 (Winter 1971), pp. 156-167.

Miller, P. M.; Hersen, M.; and Eisler, R. M. "Relative Effectiveness of Instructions, Agreements, and Reinforcement in Behavioral Contracts with Alcoholics." *Journal of Abnormal Psychology,* 83 (November 1974), pp. 548-553.

Obitz, F. W.; Wood, J. D.; and Cantergiani, N. "Alcoholics' Perceptions of Group Therapy and Alcoholics Anonymous." *British Journal of Addiction,* 72 (December 1977), pp. 321-324.

Olson, R. P. "Long-Term Effects of Behavioral Versus Insight-Oriented Therapy with Inpatient Alcoholics." *Journal of Consulting and Clinical Psychology,* 49 (December 1981), pp. 866-877.

Pattison, E. M.; Coe, R.; and Rhodes, R. J. "Evaluation of Alcoholism Treatment." *Archives of General Psychiatry,* 20 (April 1969), pp. 478-488.

Ritson, B. "Involvement in Treatment and Its Relation to Outcome Amongst Alcoholics." *British Journal of Addiction,* 64 (March 1969), pp. 23-29.

Saunders, D. N. "Prevention and Control of 'Drunk Driving': Lessons for Social Work." *Health and Social Work,* 4 (Fall 1979), pp. 84-106.

Scanlon, J. C. "Cost Saving/Benefit Analysis of Drug Abuse Treatment." *American Journal of Drug and Alcohol Abuse,* 3, No. 1 (1976), pp. 95-101.

Schramm, C. J., and DeFillippi, R. J. "Characteristics of Successful Alcoholism Treatment Programs for American Workers." *British Journal of Addiction,* 70 (September 1975), pp. 271-275.

Sheffet, A. M., et al. "Assessment of Treatment Outcomes in a Drug Abuse Rehabilitation Network: Newark, New Jersey." *American Journal of Drug and Alcohol Abuse,* 7, No. 2 (1980), pp. 141-173.

Simpson, D. D.; Savage, L. J.; and Lloyd, M. R. "Follow-Up Evaluation of Treatment of Drug Abuse During 1969 to 1972." *Archives of General Psychiatry,* 36 (July 1979), pp. 772-780.

Stead, P., and Viders, J. A. " 'SHARP' Approach to Treating Alcoholism." *Social Work,* 24 (March 1979), pp. 144-149.

Vaglum, P., and Fossheim, I. "The Results of Different Institutional Treatment Programs—Are They Different in Different Groups of Drug Abusers?" *Acta Psychiatrica Scandinavica,* 62, No. 284 (1980), pp. 21-28.

Van Dijk, W. K., and Van Dijk-Koffeman, A. "A Follow-Up Study of 211 Treated Male Alcoholic Addicts." *British Journal of Addiction,* 68 (March 1973), pp. 3-24.

Verinis, J. S. "Alcoholic Inpatients' Evaluation of Different Group Experiences." *Psychological Reports,* 46, No. 3, Part 2 (1980), pp. 1155-1158.

Vogler, R. E.; Compton, J. V.; and Weissbach, T. A. "Integrated Behavior Change Techniques for Alcoholics." *Journal of Consulting and Clinical Psychology,* 43 (April 1975), pp. 233-243.

Vogler, R. E., et al. "Electrical Aversion Conditioning with Chronic Alcoholics." *Journal of Consulting and Clinical Psychology,* 34 (June 1970), pp. 302-307.

Wood, D., et al. "Psychodrama with an Alcohol Abuser Population." *Group Psychotherapy, Psychodrama and Sociometry,* 32 (1979), pp. 75-88.

Wright, K. D., and Scott, T. B. "The Relationship of Wives' Treatment to the Drinking Status of Alcoholics." *Journal of Studies on Alcohol,* 39 (September 1978), pp. 1577-1581.

Yalom, I. D., et al. "Alcoholics in Interactional Group Therapy: An Outcome Study." *Archives of General Psychiatry,* 35 (April 1978), pp. 419-425.

Zimberg, S.; Lipscomb, H.; and Davis, E. B. "Socio-Psychiatric Treatment of Alcoholism in an Urban Ghetto." *American Journal of Psychiatry,* 127 (December 1971), pp. 106-110.

Unemployment

Appel, G. L., and Schlenker, R. E. "An Analysis of Michigan's Experience with Work Incentives." *Monthly Labor Review,* 94 (September 1971), pp. 15-22.

Azrin, N. H.; Flores, S.; and Kaplan, S. J. "Job-Finding Club: A Group-Assisted Program for Obtaining Employment." *Rehabilitation Counseling Bulletin,* 21 (December 1970), pp. 130-140.

Beck, R. B., et al. *San Antonio Rehabilitation—Welfare Report on Research and Demonstration Project RD 1513.* Austin: Texas Department of Public Welfare, 1967.

Bloomberg, C. M. "Job Training for Dropouts." *American Journal of Orthopsychiatry,* 37 (July 1967), pp. 779-786.

Cates, C. W. "Comparison of Three Mailing Approaches to Solicit Job Opportunities for Handicapped Persons." *Rehabilitation Counseling Bulletin,* 24 (June 1981), pp. 362-365.

Galvin, D. E. "Program Evaluation in Michigan VR Service." *Social and Rehabilitation Record,* 1 (October 1974), pp. 28-31.

Goldsamt, M. R. "Life Satisfaction and the Older Disabled Worker." *Journal of the American Geriatrics Society,* 15 (April 1967), pp. 394-399.

Janzen, R. V., et al. *Interpersonal Relationships: Factors in Rural Rehabilitation.* Logan: Regional Rehabilitation Research Institute, University of Utah, 1969.

Latimore, J. "Social Services in the Iron Cage." *Journal of Sociology and Social Welfare,* 6 (November 1979), pp. 756-769.

Mitchell, J. J., et al. *Implementing Welfare-Employment Programs: An Institutional Analysis of the Work Incentive (WIN) Program.* Washington, D.C.: Employment and Training Administration, The Urban Institute, 1980.

Prescott, E.; Tash, W.; and Usdane, W. "Training and Employability: Effects of MDTA on AFDC Recipients." *Welfare in Review,* 9 (January-February 1971), pp. 1-6.

Reid, W. J., and Smith, A. D. "AFDC Mothers View the Work Incentive Program." *Social Service Review,* 46 (September 1972), pp. 347-362.

Schinke, S. P., et al. "Improving Teenage Mothers' Ability to Compete for Jobs." *Social Work Research and Abstracts,* 14 (Fall 1978), pp. 25-29.

Smith, A. D.; Fortune, A. E.; and Rewid, W. J. "WIN, Work, and Welfare." *Social Service Review,* 49 (September 1975), pp. 396-404.

Treitel, R. *Benefits and Costs of Cost-Benefit Analysis of Vocational Rehabilitation Programs.* Uppsala, Sweden: World Congress of International Sociological Associations, 1978.

Ugland, R. P. "Job Seeker's Aids: A Systematic Approach for Organizing Employer Contacts." *Rehabilitation Counseling Bulletin,* 21 (December 1977), pp. 107-115.

APPENDIX

The following is by no means an inclusive list of activities or publications undertaken on this subject. For obvious reasons, it emphasizes those items that have been undertaken or published by various of the national professional organizations in social work, especially NASW.

―――*B.N.S.*

Chronology of Selected Publications and Events Related to the Definitions and Clarification of Social Work Practice

1915　　Flexner, A. "Is Social Work a Profession?" In *Proceedings of the National Conference of Charities and Correction,* pp. 576–590. Chicago: Hildeman Printing Co., 1915.

1929　　Lee, P. R. "Social Work: Cause and Function." In *Proceedings of the National Conference of Social Work,* pp. 3–20. Chicago: University of Chicago Press, 1929.

　　　　Social Casework: Generic and Specific: A Report of the Milford Conference. New York: American Association of Social Workers, 1929; reprinted by the National Association of Social Workers, 1974.

1935　　Lewin, K. "Survey of the Experimental Investigations." In Lewin, *Selected Papers: A Dynamic Theory of Personality.* New York: McGraw-Hill Book Co., 1935.

1937　　Sheffield, A. *Social Insight in Case Situations,* New York: D. Appleton-Century Co., 1937.

1947　　Pray, K. L. M. "A Restatement of the Generic Principles of Social Case Work Practice." *Social Casework,* 28 (October 1947), pp. 283–290.

1949　　Bowers. S. "The Nature and Definition of Social Casework: Part I." *Social Casework,* 30 (October 1949), pp. 311–317.

　　　　Bowers, S. "The Nature and Definition of Social Casework: Part II." *Social Casework,* 30 (November 1949), pp. 369–375.

　　　　Bowers, S. "The Nature and Definition of Social Casework: Part III." *Social Casework,* 30 (December 1949), pp. 412–417.

1951　　Hollis, E. V., and Taylor, A. D. *Social Work Education in the United States.* New York: Columbia University Press, 1951.

58 / Bibliography

1957 Greenwood, E. "Attributes of a Profession," *Social Work,* 2 (July 1957), pp. 45–55.

1958 Bartlett, H. M. "Toward Clarification and Improvement of Social Work Practice." *Social Work,* 3 (April 1958), pp. 3–9.

Boehm, W. W. "The Nature of Social Work." *Social Work,* 3 (April 1958), pp. 10–18.

Subcommittee on the Working Definition of Social Work Practice for the Commission on Social Work Practice. "Working Definition of Social Work Practice." *Social Work,* 3 (April 1958), pp. 5–8.

1959 Boehm, W. W. *Objectives of the Social Work Curriculum of the Future.* New York: Council on Social Work Education, 1959.

Child Welfare League of America. *Child Welfare as a Field of Social Work Practice.* New York: CWLA, 1959.

Council on Social Work Education. *The Curriculum Study,* 12 vols. New York: CSWE, 1959.

1960 Schwartz, M. "Toward a Working Definition of Community Organization." New York: National Association of Social Workers, 1960. Mimeographed.

1961 Bartlett, H. M. *Analyzing Social Work Practice by Fields.* New York: National Association of Social Workers, 1961.

Bartlett, H. M. *Social Work Practice in the Health Field.* New York: National Association of Social Workers, 1961.

1962 Gordon, W. E. "A Critique of the Working Definition," *Social Work,* 7 (October 1962), pp. 3–13.

Subcommittee on Fields of Practice, NASW Commission on Practice. "Identifying Fields of Practice in Social Work," *Social Work,* 7 (April 1962), pp. 7–14.

1964 Hartford, M. "A Working Definition of Social Group Work." New York: National Association of Social Workers, 1964. Mimeographed.

NASW Commission on Practice. *Building Social Work Knowledge: Report of a Conference.* New York: National Association of Social Workers, 1964.

Appendix / 59

1965   Carter, G., "Fields of Practice: Report of a Workshop." New York: National Association of Social Workers, 1965. Mimeographed.

Gordon, W. E. "Knowledge and Value: Their Distinction and Relationship to Clarifying Social Work Practice." *Social Work,* 10 (July 1965), pp. 32-39.

Gordon, W. E. "Toward a Social Work Frame of Reference." *Journal of Education for Social Work,* 1 (Fall 1965), pp. 19-26.

1969   Gordon, W. E. "Basic Concepts for an Integrative and Generative Conception of Social Work." In G. Hearn, ed., *The General Systems Approach: Contributions Toward an Holistic Conception of Social Work,* pp. 5-11. New York: Council on Social Work Education, 1969.

1970   Bartlett, H. M. *The Common Base of Social Work Practice.* New York: National Association of Social Workers, 1970.

1974   Thiemann, B., and Battle, M. "Developing a System of Social Work Specialization." Washington, D. C.: National Association of Social Workers, 1974. Mimeographed.

1977   Special Issue on Conceptual Frameworks. *Social Work,* 22 (September 1977), pp. 337-444.

1978   Conference on the Future of Social Work Research, sponsored by NASW and NIMH, October 1978, San Antonio, Texas.

1979   National Association of Social Workers-Council on Social Work Education, Task Force on Specialization. "Specialization in the Social Work Profession," *NASW News,* 24 (April 1979), pp. 21, 31.

1980   Ewalt, P. L. *Toward a Definition of Clinical Social Work.* New York: National Association of Social Workers, 1980.

Fanshel, D., *Future of Social Work Research.* Washington, D. C.: National Association of Social Workers, 1980.

1981   "Conceptual Frameworks II: Second Special Issue on Conceptual Frameworks." *Social Work,* 26 (January 1981), including C. Meyer, "Social Work Purpose: Status by Choice or Coercion," pp. 69-75, and D. Brieland, "Definition, Specialization, and Domain in Social Work," pp. 79-83.

SEP 3 0 1988